TOURISM DEVELOPMENT IN

SIKKIM

Economic Benefits & Conservation Linkages

TOURISM DEVELOPMENT IN

SIKKIM

Economic Benefits & Conservation Linkages

Dr. Iyatta M. Upreti

EXCELLER BOOKS®
A GLOBAL PRESS

TOURISM DEVELOPMENT IN SIKKIM
Economic Benefits & Conservation Linkages

Cover by Exceller Books using resources from Pixabay.com

ISBN: 978-93-48892-42-3

First published in India in 2025 by Exceller Books,
An imprint of GE Group,
G1, Dream Apartment, Degree College Road, Belgharia,
Kolkata, 700056, India
www.excellerbooks.com

EXCELLER BOOKS®
A GLOBAL PRESS

Dedicated

To

My Revered Parents

Mr. Krishna Chandra Maharana & Mrs. Kamalini Maharana

My Beloved Husband

Mr. Manoj Uprety

My Dearest Sons

Abhinandan and Abhigyan

For being a source of constant inspiration and encouragement in all my academic pursuits

Acknowledgement

I express my sincere gratitude to my supervisor, Dr. S. C. Rai, G.B. Pant Institute of Himalayan Environment and Development, for his constructive guidance and encouragement throughout the period of study. I also express my sincere thanks to my co-supervisor, Professor M. M. Jana, Department of Geography and Applied Geography, The North Bengal University, for his continuous guidance and support. I am thankful to the Director, G. B. Pant Institute of Himalayan Environment and Development, for his valuable suggestions and for providing facilities. I am very much thankful to Dr. Eklabya Sharma, Scientist-in-Charge of the Sikkim unit of the G.B. Pant Institute of Himalayan Environment and Development, for his humble guidance and creative suggestions from time to time.

I am highly grateful to Professor J.S. Singh, Department of Botany, Banaras Hindu University, for his constructive and technical suggestions, time and again. I am highly obliged to Dr. Roweny Jackson, who has been available to me from time to time for consultation and helped in statistical analysis using window-based software.

I have greatly benefited from discussions with Professor Kanchan Chopra of the Institute of Economic Growth, University of Delhi; B. Thakur, and Dr. R. B. Singh, Department of Geography, Delhi School of Economics, University of Delhi; Dr. T. R. Manoharan, Information Research System for the non-aligned and other developing countries, India Habitat Center, New Delhi and Dr. J. Gabriel Campbel, Former Asia Program Director, The Mountain Institute, U.S.A.

I express my sincere gratitude to Professor A. N. Purohit, Director, High Altitude Plant Physiology Research Center, Srinagar, Garhwal, for his kind suggestion, inspiration and support. Thanks are also due to Dr. R.

C. Sundriyal, Dr. Manju Sundriyal and Dr. Drupad Choudhary of the North East unit of G.B. Pant Institute of Himalayan Environment and Development for their suggestions and encouragement.

I would like to thank Ms. Nandita Jain, Project Manager (SBE), for all the help she rendered during the project tenure. I am indeed very much indebted to Mr. Renzino Lepcha, Project Officer, Sikkim Biodiversity and Ecotourism project and all TAAS (Travel Agent Association of Sikkim) members and community people for providing me with all the required information without hesitation.

I wish to put on record my sincere thanks to various Government Departments of the Sikkim government, especially Forest, Tourism, Agriculture, Survey and Settlements, and other organizations, the Census Directorate of Sikkim and Sikkim Government College.

Words are inadequate to express my gratitude to my parents, my uncle Mr. I. L. Uprety, Aunty Mrs. Anita Uprety, my sister and brothers, without whose constant support and help, the present work could not have materialized. I was fortunate to have the help and support of my younger brother, Swastik, during the crucial phase of writing.

The study would not have been possible without the support and cooperation of the following staff: Er. A. P. Krishna, Dr. K.K. Singh, L.K.

Rai, Dr. Y.K. Rai, Dr. Rita Sharma, Shri R.K. Das, Sabita Krishna, J. Dhakal, P.K. Tamang, Shyambir, Musafir Rai, Mohan Thapa, Arun Tamang, P. B. Chettri and Sunil Balmiki of the G.B. Pant Institute of Himalayan Environment and Development, Sikkim Unit.

I acknowledge deep gratitude and thanks to M.V.S. Manian for his technical support in the compilation, graphics and presentation. I acknowledge my friends Nakul Chettri, Alka Jain, and H. Bir Kumar Singh, who deserve special mention for their moral support, helping me through the hard times, and sharing the good times with me. Bidya Pradhan and Bhanuraj Sharma were my sole source of assistance in the field; their help and care went way beyond the call of duty. Thanks are also due to all the Yuksam and Khecheopalri communities, who provided constant moral support, without which this work would not have been possible.

Lastly, I am thankful to the Biodiversity Conservation Network under the Biodiversity Support Program (BSP), United States Agency for International Development (USAID) and IDRC Canada for their financial support.

Iyatta Maharana

Table of Contents

Glossary

ACS	Annual Consumer Surplus
BCN	Biodiversity Conservation Network
BNP	Borvli National Park
BSP	Biodiversity Support Program
CoC	Code of Conduct
CVM	Contingent Valuation Method
DBDC	Double Bounded Dichotomous Choice
FCC	False Colour Composite
FITs	Free and Independent Travellers
ft3	Cubic feet
GNP	Gross National Products
GBPIHED	G.B. Pant Institute of Himalayan Environment and Development
Ha	Hectare
ha I	Per hectare
HMI	Himalayan Mountaineering Institute
IATA	International Air Transport Association
IRS	Indian Remote Sensing
IUCN	International Union for Conservation of Nature; The World Conservation Union
IUOTO	International Union of Official Travel Organizations
KCC	Khangchendzonga Conservation Committee
KNP	Khangchendzonga National Park
Kholas/Chus	Stream
/Km^2	Per Kilometer Square
LISS	Linear Image Self Scanning
LPG	Liquid Petroleum Gas
Mg	Mega Gram (tonne)
NGOs	Non-Governmental Organizations
NTFP	Non-timber Forest Product
OLS	Ordinary Least Squires
PATA	Pacific Area Travel Association
PHC	Primary Health Centre
PLA	Participatory Learning and Action
PRA	Participatory Rural Appraisal
PTR	Perriyar Tiger Reserves
SBE	Sikkim Biodiversity and Ecotourism
SDP	State Domestic Product
TAAN	Trekking Agent Association of Nepal
TAAS	Travel Agent Association of Sikkim
TCM	Travel Cost Method

UNO	United Nations
USA	United States of America
UNCED	United Nations Commission for Environment Development
USAID	United States Agency for International Development
WTO	World Tourism Organization
WTTC	World Travel and Tourism Council
WTP	Willingness to Pay
Yr	Year
Yr	Per year

List of Tables

List of Figures and Plates

Chapter 1 | Introduction

Tourism is one of the most rapidly expanding sectors within the world's largest and fastest-growing industry, emerging as a significant sector of economic development. Since the last century, tourism has been increasing, resulting in a growing influx of people into mountain regions.

This sector remains high on the international agenda of development. The 7th session of the Commission on Sustainable Development focused on tourism, and subsequently, work programs on sustainable tourism are being developed. Also, the Convention on Biological Diversity is embarking on tourism programs, and bilateral and multilateral financial institutions have placed tourism high on their priority lists. The UN declared 2002 as the International Year of Ecotourism, and the World Tourism Organization adopted a Global Code of Ethics for Tourism at its General Assembly, held in Santiago de Chile, from September 27 until October 1, 1999 (Groth, 2000).

The majority of tourists visit places for leisure, contributing to the world's largest industry, which employs 212 million people (one-tenth of the world's workforce) with an output of US$3.4 trillion, 6% of the world's gross national product. The total global capital investments (10.7%), worldwide consumer spending (10.9%), and the world's international trade in goods and services (6.8%) make tourism one of the three top categories of trade (WTTC, 1995). Understanding its high multiplier effect, governments around the world are taking more proactive roles to attract tourists, recognizing tourism as an effective tool for economic diversification in areas where traditional industries are failing, as well as a source of foreign exchange earnings and better employment opportunities. The World Tourism Organization forecasts that there will be 702 million international arrivals in the year 2000, that arrivals will reach 1 billion in the year 2010 and that by 2020, they will reach 1.6 billion, nearly three times the number of international trips made in 1996, which was 592 million (Groth, 2000).

Travellers of the 21st century will go farther and farther. The Tourism 2020 Vision forecast predicts that by 2020, one out of every three trips will be a long-haul journey to another region of the world (Groth, 2000). The World Travel and Tourism Council (WTTC) predicts that tourism earnings by 2005 will be double its current gross income and generate 90% more jobs. Its capital investment is expected to increase threefold to US$1.7

trillion, and attract more than twice the current level of consumer spending, amounting to US$4.6 trillion.

For many developing countries, their natural environments continue to be a source of significant economic benefits, attracting international and domestic visitors who often seek an authentic natural experience, as well as, to a lesser degree, a cultural experience. Detailed information on the numbers of visitors to natural areas and the resulting economic activity in developing countries is both difficult to obtain and often unreliable. Tourism associated with natural and protected areas has been and continues to be a growing sector in the global tourism industry (Whelan, 1991; Brandon & Hawkins, 1996). Of the estimated US$55 billion in tourism receipts in the Third World, a significant portion of this in the early 1990s was the result of nature tourism activities (Whelan, 1991). Although not always concerned with protected areas, it is estimated that annual global expenditure on adventure-related travel amounts to US$110 billion (Adventure Travel Society, 1998). Perhaps it is difficult to generalize, but for many developing countries, their natural heritage is a primary attraction for both international visitors and an increasing number of domestic tourists.

Tourism development in India, given its federal character, remains a state subject and, therefore, the politics of the states concerned have a greater bearing on the aspects of policy implementation. The Eighth Five-Year Plan (1992-1997) document of India lays emphasis on the promotion of the tourism sector. The national action plan for tourism development has emphasized enhancing the socio-economic status of the people, increasing employment opportunities, diversifying the tourism product, and preserving cultural heritage and the environment.

The Hindu-Kush Himalayan region is a unique area in the world, offering rich biodiversity, diverse cultures, socio-economic traditions, history, and varied lifestyles. Since time immemorial, lofty mountain ranges of the Himalaya have attracted tourists, pilgrims, naturalists, explorers, trekkers, mountaineers, and other various adventure travellers. Tourism can play a key role in the development of the remote mountain areas. The development of tourism activities may help diversify the mountain economy and provide viable alternative livelihood opportunities for mountain people.

In view of the limited industrial growth in Sikkim, tourism can become a potential source of income generation in the remote, hilly regions, generating employment opportunities for the local community. Over recent years, this area has undergone significant changes due to the growth of tourism. Since 1990, there has been a significant increase in visitation numbers (Rai & Sundriyal, 1997). Tourism is a highly seasonal activity in the state, with October through November and March through June being the two peak seasons. The high growth rate of tourism has recently caused some serious threats to the natural environment. Most of the tourism activities in Sikkim are either in protected areas or cultural sites. Protected areas are the State properties where ownership, control and management of resources and claims rest with the government; however, usufructuary rights for tourism purposes are held by a variety of users, including local entrepreneurs, communities, commercial tour operators (residents and also from outside the area and sometimes the region) and government agencies such as the Forest and Tourism Departments. Cultural sites of tourism interest, such as monasteries and their sacred forests, are under the control of local institutions. There is a unique example of Khecheopalri Sacred Lake, where the legal rights lie with the State Government, but the operational rights seem to be with a local institution, viz. Khecheopalri Holy Lake Welfare Committee.

The problems facing the region call for the promotion of activities that are based on the region's comparative advantage, which help in the diversification of the mountain economy, provide alternative livelihood opportunities for the local people, and, at the same time, actively promote environmental care so that the twin issues of economic development and environmental degradation can be simultaneously addressed. Tourism in the mountains has the potential to address all these concerns and provide alternative, environmentally friendly income and employment opportunities throughout the region.

As concern grows over the loss of natural heritage in the area, it appears that this is an ideal time to facilitate ecologically and socially responsible tourism at key destinations, thereby conserving the biological diversity of the area. Therefore, the present study was undertaken to provide robust empirical evidence on the environmental, economic and social impacts of tourism, and attempts are being made to make tourism environmentally friendly, and involve local communities as promising stakeholders so that they can get direct benefits from the tourists and at the same time protect the biodiversity and cultural heritage of the area.

1.1. The Sikkim Biodiversity and Ecotourism Project

The "Sikkim Biodiversity and Ecotourism (SBE) project" was supported by the Biodiversity Conservation Network (BCN) under the Biodiversity Support Program (BSP), USAID. The project was a collaborative effort of the G.B. Pant Institute of Himalayan Environment and Development, the Mountain Institute, USA, the Travel Agent Association of Sikkim, the Green Circle, and local NGOs working with communities, implemented in the West District of Sikkim. The Government of Sikkim has also played a key role at the various stages of the project implementation. The Project's overall objective is to "develop viable ecotourism enterprises at the key destinations in Sikkim which provide sustained incentives and support for local communities and the Sikkimese tourism industry to effectively protect and enhance the high biodiversity found at these sites and the state as a whole." The project aimed to support community-based enterprise development approaches for the conservation of Sikkim's unique biological diversity, serving as a collaborative initiative designed to conserve the biological diversity of key destinations in Sikkim. The specific objectives of the project were:

- To increase the interest and capacity of local communities, tour operators and local NGOs to initiate and implement effective participatory biodiversity conservation of the project sites,
- To increase market demand for Travel Agents Association of Sikkim (TAAS) and community member ecotourism products,
- To improve the quality and diversity of the ecotourism products offered by local communities and TAAS members and the returns to investment and labor,
- To improve the policy environment and knowledge base for the development of more effective biodiversity conservation and ecotourism linkages, and
- To plan monitoring and applied research, which included planning and policy development, enterprise monitoring, socio-economic monitoring, biodiversity monitoring and community resource management research.

The present piece of work was undertaken as part of monitoring and applied research in two destinations, viz. Yuksam-Dzongri-Goechha La trekking corridor and Sacred Khecheopalri Lake to increase knowledge of the key relationship between economic benefits and conservation through tourism development.

1.2. Core Hypotheses

- The effectiveness of biodiversity conservation (forest) is closely related to the degree to which local people obtain direct and indirect economic benefits from tourism and are well informed on environmental issues and conservation activities.
- Ecotourism activities will lead to an increase in revenue from tourism-related activities for stakeholder groups and local households directly or indirectly involved in the tourism sector.

1.3. Objectives

- To study and compare the relationships between tourism growth, market trends and tourism-related revenue distribution patterns in two sites.
- To assess and identify possible interventions that strengthen the capabilities of local people and local communities to derive maximum employment and income benefits from tourism.
- To identify mechanisms used for increasing entrepreneurial skills and capacities to expand resources among local stakeholders involved in ecologically sound and socially responsible ecotourism and other development activities.

1.4. Design of the Thesis

The present study is divided into seven chapters, each dealing with varied yet interrelated aspects. Chapter one provides an introductory outline of the tourism, hypothesis and objectives. Chapter two introduces the review of literature, indicating the chronological development and changing content of the concept. Since not much study has been carried out on the topic in the Indian context, more attention is paid to review studies carried out in other countries, particularly in developed countries. In addition, an attempt has been made here to review some of the specific valuation studies on non-marketed commodities. The third chapter is devoted to describing the study area, which encompasses the physical, cultural, and infrastructure settings. The dynamics of tourism, visitor profiles, nature and characteristics of tourism, tourist products, and tourist reactions have been examined in the fourth chapter. It is followed by an appraisal of human resources and socio-economic development (Chapter 5). The economic evaluation of environmental damage to natural ecosystems is discussed in chapter six, which is carried out using the travel cost method (TCM) and the contingent valuation method (CVM). In addition to this, the nature and extent of dependency of stakeholder groups on KNP and the Lake area are also described in this chapter. The tourism sector, its economic significance, and the participation of government and non-government agencies in tourism and environmental conservation are described in chapter seven. It recapitulates as a prelude the observations made in preceding chapters and suggests a requisite planning. Keeping in view the defined objectives, some relevant aspects of planning for tourism development in mountain regions have been critically examined prior to the formulation of an integrated framework. The end of the study is marked by a summary of basic elements and references.

1.5. Limitations

The following are some of the important limitations of the present study:

- The major constraint was the inaccessibility of the area due to steep slopes in many parts of the trekking corridor. Unpredicted weather conditions and natural hazards, such as landslides, continuous rain, and extreme cold weather, disrupted the work plan, and the schedule was often missed or covered later.
- The TCM technique is applied to estimate the ecotourism value of visitors from Sikkim State only. The consumer surplus of visitors from other states and abroad may generally be higher than the estimated amount. The travel cost method can be applied to foreign tourists, but its implementation at both sites has been hindered by budgetary constraints. In both sites, most of the visits from abroad are part of multiple destination trips. The economic value of such recreational visits cannot be estimated using the simple travel cost method.
- The sites possess some unique recreational characteristics, and the value of specific characteristics, such as the viewing value of the Red Panda, butterflies, and other wild animals, as well as the value of the trekking experience, is not separately estimated. There are certain methods, such as the Hedonic Travel Cost Method, to estimate the

recreation value of such specific characteristics, but that has not been applied in this study.

- There is very little secondary information related to research available for tourism. Tourism activities are highly seasonal and operate only in two seasons.
- Indigenous items of tourism interest are not properly marketed by local communities, tour operators and government.
- Very little information is available on government regulations related to protected area management where tourism is operative.
- Planning is totally devoid of local control, and programs are irrelevant to the local environment.
- There is a lack of investment potential locally, and a concerted effort by the government to induce local investments.
- There is a lack of proper tourism policy and institutional development.
- The Indian subcontinent is one of the ten mega-biodiversity centres of the World. The eastern Himalayan region is the most significant biodiversity hotspot in the Indian subcontinent, harbouring the largest number of endemics and endangered species (Khoshoo, 1992). Khangchendzonga National Park and the Khecheopalri Lake area in Sikkim are very important biodiversity-oriented tourist destinations. Therefore, this study focuses on the economic benefits and conservation-linked tourism development in the western part of Sikkim, encompassing the above two destinations.

Chapter 2 | The Story So Far

2.1. Evolution of Tourism

The term "tourist", meaning "an individual who travels for the pleasure of travelling, out of curiosity", made its first appearance around 1800 (Ceballos-Lascurain, 1996). However, the origins of this activity go back considerably further. Humankind has always had the desire to travel, to visit exotic places and to encounter different cultures. In the 18th and 19th centuries, the "Grand Tour" became extremely fashionable among European aristocrats as a means of adventure and discovery, marking a shift in motivations for travel. However, tourism did not become more accessible to the population in general until the time of the Industrial Revolution (Wood & House, 1991). During this time, a considerable amount of travel for pleasure was essentially a quest for spectacular scenery. This was the beginning of travel for pleasure and of the transformation of travel into tourism. The era of organized tourism had started (Sarkar & Dhar, 1998). This period also witnessed the first serious environmental impacts attributable to tourism.

Early in the century, by which time summer holidays were taken regularly by Europeans and Americans, improvements in international and intra-national tourist facilities, especially the introduction of chartered flights, and increasingly cheaper and varied tourist attractions further stimulated and provided essential conditions for the growth of tourism. However, by about this time, tourism had started to earn itself a very bad name due to thoughtless development and the disruption of local cultures, values, and economies. During the birth of mass international travel, beginning in the late 1940s, and continuing through most of the 1960s, tourism was often regarded as a panacea for developing countries, which could raise foreign exchange earnings, GNP and tax revenue, and also increase employment. However, growth in public concern about the environment and the negative impacts of mass tourism ultimately led to a reexamination of this notion. Purported economic benefits from tourism came under harsh scrutiny, and recognition of the problems involved in measuring the economic benefits of tourism led to increased analysis of its costs (Lawrence, 1992). At the same time, conservation organizations were formed to lobby governments to set aside land not just for the enjoyment of tourists, or for the sake of showy animals, but to preserve the natural integrity of whole ecosystems.

After the Second World War, for the first time, tourism was viewed as an engine for economic development. This led governments to assume responsibility for promoting tourism. Official tourist organizations at the national level were established in most European countries. Considering the international character of tourism, the post-war years also witnessed the emergence of several international organizations focused on travel and tourism. Among them were the International Union of Official Travel Organisations (IUOTO), now an intergovernmental agency called the World Tourism Organisation (UNWTO); the International Air Transport Association (IATA); and the Pacific Area Travel Association (PATA). India was among the first developing countries to become a member of IUOTO in 1951 (Sarkar & Dhar, 1998).

2.2. Nature-Based Tourism and Ecotourism

Nature tourism refers to all tourism that is directly dependent on the use of natural resources in a relatively undeveloped state, including scenery, topography, water features, vegetation, and wildlife. Thus, it includes hunting, countryside motorbiking, and white-water rafting, even if the use of the natural resources by the tourist is neither wise nor sustainable (Butler, 1992; Healy, 1992; Ceballos-Lascurain, 1996). Like traditional tourism, it can be negatively influenced by various external factors. This accounts for its instability as a source of income. Nevertheless, nature-based tourism (which includes ecotourism) is a rapidly growing sector of the tourism economy. Its global value for 1988 has been estimated to be as high as US$1 trillion (Filion et al., 1992). It has often proved to be a powerful incentive for conservation in all parts of the world. However, at the same time, uncontrolled mass tourism has and continues to contribute to the degradation of many areas of natural and cultural significance, resulting in the loss of biological and cultural diversity, as well as important sources of income. Clearly, what is needed is an environmentally responsible approach to tourism or "sustainable tourism".

Sustainable tourism, as defined by Ceballos-Lascurain (1996), is "tourism that is developed and managed in such a way that all tourism activity which in some way focuses on a heritage resource (be it natural or cultural) can continue indefinitely". In other words, it does not detract from efforts to maintain that resource in perpetuity (FNNPE 1992). Sustainable tourism is the broadest descriptor employed to denote all types of tourism, whether based on natural or human-made resources, that contribute to sustainable development (Healy, 1992).

In recent years, a specific category of nature-based tourism has developed along these lines. "Ecological tourism" or "Ecotourism" as defined by IUCN's Ecotourism Program is "environmentally responsible travel and visitation to relatively undisturbed natural areas, in order to enjoy and appreciate nature that promotes conservation, has low visitor impacts, and provides for beneficially active socio-economic involvement of local population" (Ceballos-Lascurain, 1993). The definition of Ecotourism Society is similar, which is: "ecotourism refers to responsible travel to natural areas that conserve the environment and sustain the well-being of local people" (Boo, 1990; Blangy & Wood, 1992; Lindberg & Hawkins, 1993; Hvenegaard & Dearden, 1998). Studies documenting the association between ecotourism and conservation, though limited, have intensified recently. On the supply side, efforts have focused on potential sites for ecotourism (Boyd et al., 1994), environmental impacts (Johnson et al., 1996), local communities (Brockelman & Dearden, 1990), and planning (Nelson, 1994). On the demand side, researchers have explored economic impacts (Tobian & Mendelsohrr, 1991), marketing (Wight, 1994), and characteristics of ecotourists (Weiler & Richins, 1995). Studies evaluating ecotourism's achievement of specific conservation and development principles are also beginning to emerge (Lindberg et al., 1996; Wallace & Pierce, 1996).

Farrel & Runyan (1991) distinguished between nature tourism and ecotourism by describing the latter as "more exclusively purposeful and focused on the enhancement or maintenance of natural systems". Thus, we can distinguish between, for example, traditional tour operators and principled ecotourism operators. The former frequently show no commitment to conservation or natural area management, merely offering clients an opportunity to experience exotic places and people before they change or disappear. Ecotourism operators, on the other hand, have begun to form partnerships with protected area managers and local people, with the intention of contributing to the long-term protection of natural resources and local development, and in the hope of improving mutual understanding between hosts and visitors (Wallace, 1992).

Ecotourism is reliant on natural phenomena in relatively undisturbed sites (Boyed et al., 1994), such as protected areas. Before being promoted, the impacts of ecotourism must be thoroughly examined in the context of a protected area's mandate. Tour operators often refer to themselves as "ecotourism" operators, with varying standards for conservation and development goals. However, monitoring has been proposed recently for some jurisdictions (Allcock et al., 1994).

Economically, ecotourism can impact the sustainability of natural resource use at ecotourism sites in several ways (Steele, 1995).

- First, ecotourism may generate higher economic returns than other resource activities (Threshers, 1981; Tobias & Mendelsohn, 1991).
- Second, ecotourism benefits local economies, providing an incentive to ensure the sustainable use of biodiversity (McNeely, 1988; McNeely & Dobias, 1991). However, local expenditures can be seasonal, inflationary, transitory, or sensitive to political or economic situations (Groom et al., 1991; Wells, 1993).
- Third, these economic benefits may serve as a stimulus for the establishment of protected areas (Ceballos-Lascurian, 1996; Dabrowslci, 1994; Sewell et al., 1989).
- Finally, ecotourists may contribute to the conservation and management of ecotourism sites through mechanisms such as entry fees and donations (Wallace & Pierce, 1996).

2.3. Mountain Tourism

Tourism is the most important non-farm activity in the Inountain areas. The growth of population and the increasing demand at individual level for various non-farm items have expanded the demands for goods beyond the traditional technological practices of hill communities. The lack of adequate linkages with markets outside has also led to stagnation in farm level activities. This has necessitated the search for non-farm occupations. Tourism is one of the prime sectors that can support more people, if carefully planned and well worked economic "niche" are created (Sreedhar 1995 a & b).

The UNCED's Agenda 21, chapter 13 identified tourism as one of the key activities to provide alternative livelihood opportunities to mountain people in the process of attaining sustainable Inountain development (Keating 1993). The fragility of High Mountain environment and their vulnerability to outside disturbance is well documented (Price 1981 and Poore 1992). Over the last 20 to 40 years, mountaineering and trekking have inflicted significant impacts upon alpine and sub-alpine landscapes in many parts of the Himalaya (Pawson et al. 1984; Karan & Mather 1985; Banskota & Upadhyay 1991; Stevens et al. 1991; Wells et al. 1991; Singh 1992; Price 1992; Sarkar 1994; Price et al. 1997 and Rai & Sundriyal 1997).

Zurick (1992), in his study, analyzed adventure travel in Nepal and places it within the theoretical frameworks of tourism models and sustainable development. Building on core-periphery tourism theory, an adventure travel spatial linkage model was proposed that connect Nepal's remote frontiers with the global economy. Stevens (1993) in his study on tourism, change, and continuity in the Mount Everest Region, Nepal, examined the increasing role of tourism in the Sherpa economy and assessed changes in land-use, environment and culture. Increasing regional differentiation in wealth, inflation, out-migration, and changes in pastoralism and forest use may have long adverse effects. Shackley (1994) argued that despite the strict enforcement of environmental regulations it was clear that the cultural carrying capacity of Lo has already been exceeded with minimal economic benefits to local people. Broadus et al. (1987), Sreedhar (1995 a & b) and Sharma (1997) have argued on economic benefits for mountain communities on the development of tourism in mountain regions. However, despite this there has been no structured analysis of the merits of tourism related activity was done.

Mountain tourism has been an area long neglected in the National Tourism Agenda of India. The limited tourism growth that has occurred in the country was largely an outcome of pilgrim traffic and extension of road networks into the hills. Private initiatives were also restricted in the past by rigid controls. It is only in the last decades that the government has recognized tourism as an industry and has setup a high power committee to promote the sector.

2.3. Economic Value of Ecotourism

Tourism is the most important non-farm activity in the mountain areas. The growth of population and the increasing demand at the individual level for various non-farm items have expanded the demand for goods beyond the traditional technological practices of hill communities. The lack of adequate linkages with markets outside has also led to stagnation in farm-level activities. This has necessitated the search for non-farm occupations. Tourism is one of the prime sectors that can support more people, if a carefully planned and well-worked economic "niche" is created (Sreedhar 1995a & b).

The UNCED's Agenda 21, Chapter 13, identified tourism as one of the key activities to provide alternative livelihood opportunities for mountain people in the process of achieving sustainable mountain development (Keating, 1993). The fragility of the High Mountain environment and its vulnerability to outside disturbance are well documented (Price, 1981; Poore, 1992). Over the last 20 to 40 years, mountaineering and trekking have inflicted significant impacts upon alpine and sub-alpine landscapes in many parts of the Himalaya (Pawson et al., 1984; Karan & Mather, 1985; Banskota & Upadhyay, 1991; Stevens et al., 1991; Wells et al., 1991; Singh, 1992; Price, 1992; Sarkar, 1994; Price et al., 1997; Rai & Sundriyal, 1997).

Zurick (1992), in his study, analyzed adventure travel in Nepal and placed it within the theoretical frameworks of tourism models and sustainable development. Building on core-periphery tourism theory, an adventure travel spatial linkage model was proposed that connects Nepal's remote frontiers with the global economy. Stevens (1993), in his study on tourism, change, and continuity in the Mount Everest Region, Nepal, examined the increasing role of tourism in the Sherpa economy and assessed changes in land use, environment, and culture. Increasing regional differentiation in wealth, inflation, out-migration, and changes in pastoralism and forest use may have long-term adverse effects. Shackley (1994) argued that, despite the strict enforcement of environmental regulations, it was clear that the cultural carrying capacity had already been exceeded with minimal economic benefits to local people. Broadus et al. (1987), Sreedhar (1995a & b), and Sharma (1997) have argued on economic benefits for mountain communities on the development of tourism in mountain regions. However, despite this, no structured analysis of the merits of tourism-related activity has been done.

Mountain tourism has been an area long neglected in the National Tourism Agenda of India. The limited tourism growth that has occurred in the country was largely a result of pilgrim traffic and the extension of road networks into the hills. Private initiatives were also restricted in the past by rigid controls. It is only in the last few decades that the government has recognized tourism as an industry and established a high-level committee to promote the sector.

2.3.1. Economic Valuation of Ecosystem Services

The economic valuation of natural ecosystems is very limited in developing countries. Although numerous studies have been conducted on the topic, the majority have been carried out in developed countries. Here, an attempt is made to review only the important studies on the topic, which are relevant to the present work.

The Clawson-Knetsch (1966) uses travel-related expenditures as a reflection of the recreational value, which an individual places on a protected area. The travel cost method has been widely used due to its appealing application of observed consumer behaviour. Walsh et al. (1978) employed the contingent valuation method to estimate the value of recreational benefits of improved water quality in the South Platte River Basin in Colorado. The viability of the fish population was selected as the key characteristic for the contingent valuation study: the study estimated option, existence, and bequest values. The recreation use value was estimated at US$56 per household, whereas the option value for the same was US$22. To estimate the existence values, the respondents were asked to state their willingness to pay for the benefit. The existence value estimates for the user and non-user households were found to be US$34 and US$25, respectively. The respective bequest value estimates for these categories were US$33 and US$17. Bouwes & Schneider (1979) measured recreational trips to Pike Lake, Wisconsin, as a result of a change in water quality measured by Uttormark's Lake Condition Index (LCI), applying the travel cost method. They estimated the total mean annual consumer surplus to be US$8,5721, and the aggregate benefit was US$730,103.

Brookshire et al. (1983) conducted a study using CVM to estimate the economic value of big-horn sheep and grizzly bears in Wyoming. The grizzly bear was an endangered species, and its hunting had been prohibited. Questionnaires were distributed to local residents to elicit the respondents' willingness to pay for hypothetical future permits to hunt big horn sheep and grizzly bears. It was estimated that the range of hunting bids was between US$IO and US$30 per respondent. They also estimated the existence and observation values (the economic value for viewing wildlife species) from the questionnaire. The observation option bids in the open vicinity were estimated at US$20 for both animals. The existence value estimates for big horn sheep and grizzly bear were US$7 and US$15, respectively. The study gives evidence that the non-use values are as significant as use values.

Desvougas et al. (1987) conducted a CVM study to estimate the value of improved water quality in the Monongahelia River in Pennsylvania.

The estimated option value per household was in the range of US$10 to US$38. The existence value for users and non-users of the specified non-market good was US$66 and US$42, respectively. Henry et al. (1988) estimated benefits associated with specified improvements of water quality on Lake Bemidji, Minnesota, using contingent valuation techniques. The estimated benefit of improved quality was US$88. Arge & Shogren (1989) conducted another study to estimate the per square-foot value of Lakeshore property associated with a qualitative increase in water quality from boating/fishing levels to a swimming/drinking level. All residents who own lakefront property on the east and west lakes of Okoboji, Iowa, have taken a sample unit. The estimated benefit per square foot was US$11.

Brown & Henry (1989) estimated the viewing value of elephants on safaris in Kenya by employing both travel cost and contingent valuation methods. Based on the data collected from safari tourists, a demand curve for recreational use was derived, and the consumer surplus for safaris was estimated. The study revealed that the loss of elephants will directly affect the number of visitors to the park. Dixon & Sherman (1990), in their study in Khao Yai National Park, Thailand, advocate the application of the travel cost and contingent valuation method. These methods are widely applied in estimating the economic value of non-market goods and services.

Tobias & Mendelsohn (1991) and Monkhaus & Lober (1996) estimated the value of ecotourism in a tropical rainforest reserve in Costa Rica by applying the travel cost method. The study provides the first published estimates of the value of a tropical rainforest in a developing nation. It was estimated that the recreational value of the reserve for domestic users was US$35 per visit, and it generated an annual value between US$97,500 and

US$116,200. By including foreign tourists at the same rate, the site would generate an additional value of US$400 to US$500 thousand annually. Per hectare, the recreational value of that area is about US$250. This value is several times higher than the price given to acquire the nearby lands of the protected area for expansion.

Maille & Mendelsohn (1993) estimated the value of ecotourism per foreign visitor who visits a tropical forest reserve in Madagascar using the travel cost method. The per-visitor consumer surplus was estimated at US$276 and US$360, respectively. Navrud & Mungatana (1994) estimated the environmental and recreational value of wildlife viewing in Lake Nakuru National Park in Kenya. This study revealed that the travel cost and contingent valuation methods could be successfully applied to value natural resources in developing countries. The annual recreational value of wildlife viewing in the park was found to be US$7.5 to 15 million. They emphasized the challenge for developing countries to realize their full economic potential, as well as the importance of conserving wildlife.

Munasinghe (1993) concluded that non-market valuation techniques can provide useful information for the economic evaluation of national parks, and the results of such valuation can be incorporated more fully in benefit-cost analysis, including conservation components, to determine their viability. He used an entirely different method in his valuation study. The results of opportunity cost and contingent valuation analysis were remarkably similar (US$91 and US$108 per household per year). The estimates of tourist benefits based on the travel cost and contingent valuation method were somewhat more disparate (US$24 versus US$65 per trip). Costanza et al. (1997) estimated the current economic value of 17 ecosystem services for 16 biomes. For the entire biosphere, the value (most of which was outside the market) was estimated to be in the range of US$16-54 trillion per year, with an average of US$33 trillion.

Loomis & Ekstrand (1998), in their study on the Mexican spotted owl, explored the sources and patterns of respondents' uncertainty regarding their willingness to pay and presented alternative approaches for incorporating this uncertainty into the estimation of the logit model. A regression model was used to determine the significant determinants of respondent uncertainty.

In developing countries like India, the economic valuation of the natural ecosystems is very limited. Murthy & Menkhuas (1994) first conducted a study on the economic aspects of wildlife protection in Keoladeo National Park, Bharatpur, Rajasthan State, India. The main objective of the study was to evaluate the application of recent techniques used in wildlife economics in the context of developing countries and to propose possible policy options for using economics to improve people-park relations in India. Open-ended questions were used for the survey, which simply asked the respondents: "How much would you be willing to pay?" The CVM estimates showed that the average willingness to pay per person for non-use value was Rs 519 and Rs 495 in the domestic and foreign groups, respectively. The costs and benefits of the park during 1992-93 were first estimated, and distributional weights were derived for a 10-year benefit-cost flow.

Manoharan (1996) conducted a study on the economics of the protected areas of the Periyar Tiger Reserve (PTR) in Kerala, India. The Periyar Tiger Reserve is one of the well-known Indian protected areas for nature tourism. The economic valuation of PTR has been examined within a benefit-cost analysis framework. He used the concept of total economic value to enumerate and quantify the total benefits. The total cost of the PTR was estimated at Rs 88.18 million, of which the direct cost was Rs 19.13 million, accounting for only 22% of the total cost. The opportunity cost was estimated as Rs 69.06 million. The benefit-cost ratio was 1.30.

Hadker et al. (1997) conducted another study to examine the willingness to pay function for the Bor National Park of Maharashtra, India. The study was conducted to survey the residents of Bombay and elicit their willingness to pay for the maintenance and preservation of the park using the contingent valuation techniques. The CV method has come under considerable criticism due to biases that are either inherent to or generated by the survey process. The study acknowledges these issues and adopts techniques to either circumvent or minimize them. The study gave proper attention to hypothetical bias, starting-point bias, embedding effects, and part-whole biases. The authors argue that, indeed, it is possible to improve the quality of a CV by using special surveys as well as statistical techniques so that CV results can be used for the purpose of realistic decision-making.

Chapter 3 | Understanding Sikkim

3.1. Introduction

Situated within the eastern Himalayan biogeographic zone, Sikkim, as a whole, is an attractive destination for tourists. It has a mountainous terrain where two major livelihood options, namely farming and tourism, are prevalent. Several factors influence the regional development process of any area, including physical, cultural, and infrastructure facilities and amenities, which provide a platform for various human activities. This triological frame of visualization helps comprehend the perception of a given environment. In the study area, these processes have played a significant role in shaping the various patterns of development. Their varied forms and ways have contributed to the growth and development of Sikkim as a centre of tourist attraction. Therefore, a brief appraisal of the important constituents of the study area has been presented in the pages to follow. For convenience, the whole chapter has been divided into three subparts: (i) Physical setting, (ii) Cultural setting, and (iii) Institution and infrastructure.

3.2. Geographical Location

Himalaya is one of the youngest and greatest mountain systems of the world, stretching almost 2500 km east-west. The Himalayan ranges are between 240 and 340 km wide and rise from low-lying Indian plains to over 8000 m. Sikkim, situated in the eastern Himalayan biogeographic zone, became the 22nd state of India. Only a few areas in the world offer such a unique blend of breath-taking natural beauty and rich cultural diversity, socio-economic traditions, history, and lifestyles as the north-eastern Himalayan region. From time immemorial, these lofty mountain ranges have attracted people - pilgrims, ascetics, naturalists, explorers and the like - from far and wide. In the contemporary context, tourism in the Himalayan region is a manifestation of the region's comparative advantage in pleasure and sightseeing, trekking, mountaineering, and cultural tourism.

Sikkim or Sukhim (Sukhim means New House) is a tiny state with an area of 7096 km2 (0.22% of the total geographical area of India) and a population of 405505, with an average density of 57 persons per km in 1991. The state extends between 270 4/ 46 to 280 7/ 481/ N and 880 581/ to 880 55/ 25/1 E. It is bounded on the west by Nepal, on the north by Tibet, on the east by Bhutan and Tibet, and with the Darjeeling district of West Bengal stretching along its southern boundary. The state is situated in the most magnificent range of snow-capped mountains, home to the World's third-highest mountain peak, Khanchendzonga (8598m). Other important peaks in the Khangchendzonga range are Kabru (7338m), Siniolchu (6887m), Simvo (6811m), Pandim (6691m), Jopuno (5936m) and Narsing (5825m), which are the main attractions to trekkers (Plate 1a). The area represents the main nature tour destinations and is all adjacent to biologically significant national parks or sanctuaries (Fig. 3. l). Sikkim is widely acknowledged as India's most significant biodiversity "Hot Spot" (Kumar, 1993; Shenga, 1994) and one of the most critical centres of biodiversity and endemism (Myers, 1990; WCMC, 1992) with 81 species of mammals, 550 species of birds, 650 species of butterflies, 33 species of reptiles, 16 species of amphibians, 48 species of fishes, 550 species of orchids, 36 species of rhododendrons, 4500 species of flowering plants and 175 species of wild edible plants. Apart from that, the region is home to sacred lakes, monasteries, and cultural heterogeneity, featuring distinctive ethnic groups, including the Lepchas, Bhutias, Nepalese, Limbus, and Tibetan refugees, who reside in this culturally and historically rich area (Rai, 1992). They have different festivals, dances and ways of living (food habits, marriage system and dresses).

Two sites have been selected for detailed studies: Yuksam Dzongri-Goechha La, which is used for trekking and mountaineering courses, and Khecheopalri Lake, which is used for recreation and pilgrimage. These sites represent the main nature tour destinations in Sikkim and are all adjacent to biologically significant Khangchendzonga National Park (KNP) (Fig. 3.2). KNP falls in the north and west districts of Sikkim. It was designated as a national park in August 1977, with a total area of 850 km. The area was originally under reserve forest status prior to the designation as a national park. In 1996, the area of this national park was expanded to 1,784 km^2 (25.14% of the total geographical area of Sikkim), recognizing its importance for its diverse habitats and rich floral and faunal diversity. Many villages, such as Yuksam, Sakyong, Chungthang, Mensithang, Lachen and Monguthang surrounding the park, depend on the park's natural resources for subsistence living (Fig. 3.2). The central government has recently (February 2000) included more areas in this park and designated it as a biosphere reserve. Most of the areas in the buffer zone of the biosphere have been identified for ecotourism and are also accessible to the villagers. The topography and the peaks, along with the forest wilderness in the park areas, form the main attraction of KNP.

3.2.1. Yuksam-Dzongri-Goechha La Trekking Corridor

The Yuksam-Dzongri-Goechha La trekking corridor is a 45 km long trek located in the south-western part of Khangchendzonga National Park (Fig. 3.2). The entire area, right from Khangchendzonga to the Yuksam lowlands, is considered to be sacred by the Sikkimese Buddhists according to the sacred text Nysol. The area below Mount Khangchendzonga in West Sikkim, referred to as Demojong (the hidden valley of rice), is the most sacred of all, being the abode of deities (Fig. 3.3). The Northern half of the KNP is in a restricted zone and therefore this part is not accessible to visitors. Entry into the park is allowed only with a valid permit, which is for 15 days for foreign tourists. On this trail, Yuksam is the only settled habitation, with 11 villages, 274 households, and a total population of 1572. The last village, with 9 households, is located 16 km away from Yuksam at Tshoka, on the trail, and has a total population of 59 people (Tibetan refugees) (Plate 1b). The most dominant ethnic group in Yuksam is the Limbu, followed by Bhutia, Lepcha, Nepali and Tibetan refugees. Most of them pursue traditional agricultural livelihoods. Some have associated themselves with tourism-related activities in recent years. Approximately 110 people work as porters for the tourist trek. 8 families have lodges/hotels, 25 families rear Yaks/Dzos to provide pack animals, and 6 individuals are trained local guides.

3.2.2. Sacred Khecheopalri Lake

The Khecheopalri Lake is renowned as a "Wish-Fulfilling Lake" and is considered the most sacred by the people of Sikkim. Folklore and many legends are associated with its formation and shape. The lake water is used for rites and rituals only. A Khecheopalri lake festival takes place during March every year, when a large number of local pilgrims visit the lake.

Fishing and any other recreational activities on the lake are strictly prohibited. A strong belief prevails among the community that any disturbance on the holy lake may bring calamities and unwelcome events. This lake is situated amidst pristine forest at an altitude of 1700 m (270 22/ 241/ 'N and 880 12/ 301/ E) in the West District of Sikkim (Fig. 3.2 Plate 1c). The lake represents the original "neve" region of an ancient hanging glacier, with the depression formed by the glacier's scooping action (Raina, 1966). The lake is surrounded by a broad-leaved mixed temperate forest and has a catchment area of 12 km, with 72 households and 440 persons living within it. The Lepcha is the main ethnic group in the Khecheopalri area. Traditional agriculture is the main livelihood, and recently, some households have been engaged in tourism. The influx of tourists is high, with visible impacts on the lake and its watershed. Besides visitors, communities also exploit natural resources of the lake watershed by the extraction of fuel, fodder and timber, and by livestock grazing. The lake is also a resting place for Trans-Himalayan migratory birds and supports commercial and recreational tourism.

3.3. Physical Setting

3.3.1. Physiography

A major part of the area is hilly, rising from an elevation of about 1785m near Yuksam and 8548m in Khangchendzonga. The topography progressively becomes rugged from south towards north. The northern part of the area is dominated by very steeply sloping surfaces (more than 50%) and deep cut gorges, valleys, and perpetual snow, with numerous "Kholas" or "Chus". The area has a number of glacial lakes in the higher reaches. These are sacred lakes. The Rathongchu, itself a sacred river (Plate 1d), is said to have its source in nine holy lakes closer to the mountain peaks in the higher elevation. Moreover, the river in the Yuksam region is itself considered to have 109 hidden lakes (Ramakrishnan, 1996). The Rathongchu River constitutes the major drainage system and is the focus of religious rituals. Minor streams, viz., Chockchu, Rangchu and Prekchu, feed Rathongchu. Rathongchu River and its tributaries are a striking example of a hanging valley. This hangs about 600m above the bed of Rathongchu (Pascoe, 1964). The extreme northern part of the study sites is covered by snow throughout the year and features two important glaciers: East Rathong and Onglakthang. Both glaciers are reported to be retreating rapidly.

3.3.2. Geology

Geologically, the study sites are located in the Lesser Himalayan Zone. Three important groups of rocks have been recorded at both sites, namely the Darjeeling Group, the Daling Group, and the Gondwana Group. The other group, i.e., Lingtse gneiss, occurs only as a thick linear band across the Rangit River (GSI, 1984). A major part of the area is chiefly made up of Darjeeling gneiss. The upper part of the area is covered with snow throughout the year.

The Darjeeling Group comprises chiefly high-grade gneiss containing quartz and feldspar with streaks of biotite. Besides gneiss, quartzite, sandstone, dolomite and shale are also found. A streaky, sheared granite, gneiss known as Lingtse Gneiss occurs as a NE-SW trending strip of rocks in the central and eastern part of the area (GSI, 1984).

3.3.3. Climate

The region exhibits all the characteristics of a mountain climate, where location, aspect, and altitude are of prime importance in determining the climate of a locality. The climate varies from tropical in the valleys to snowfields and glaciers at higher altitudes. The climate of the area is monsoonic and divisible into three seasons, viz., rainy (June to October), winter (November to February), and summer (March to May). Sikkim receives an average annual rainfall that varies from 1300 mm (at about 300m elevation) to 4300 mm (above 2000m elevation), and 60-75% of this rainfall is recorded during the monsoon season, i.e., June to September. The average maximum temperature at this time varies from 21° to 37°C, and the average minimum temperature from 13° to 23°C. The humidity remains high during this period (85-97%) (Rai & Sundriyal, 1997).

Temperature and rainfall data were recorded for three climatic zones in the Yuksa-Dzongri-Goechha La corridor during the study period.

The three weather stations were located at Yuksam (1700 m), Tshoka (3000 m) and Dzongri (3900 m). These locations were selected keeping in mind the three ecological zones: temperate, sub-alpine, and alpine. The major portion of the area experiences a temperate climate, where the mean temperature varies from 3.8°C in January to 24°C in August. The sub-alpine ecological zone was a bit cooler with a maximum temperature of 16.1°C (September) and a minimum of -30°C (January). The Alpine zone was under snow cover for at least five months (November to March). Hence, the maximum and minimum temperatures were recorded as 13°C (August-September) and -8°C (January), respectively (Figure 3.4).

The distribution of rainfall also follows the topographical trends. At Yuksam, the mean annual rainfall is approximately 3760 mm, while Tshoka and Dzongri experience respectively 3648 mm and 2319 mm of rainfall (Figure 3.4). The maximum rainfall was recorded during the month of August at all the locations.

The other study site, Khecheopalri Lake, falls within a temperate belt, with a maximum temperature ranging from 4°C in January to 24°C in July and August during the 1997-1998 period. Minimum temperature varied between 2.7°C in January and 17°C in August in the same period. The average annual precipitation was 3899 mm in 1997 and 3776 mm in 1998. The temporal distribution of rainfall and temperatures during 1997 and 1998 is presented in figure 3.5.

3.3.4. Soils and Vegetation

The area is endowed with diversified natural vegetation. Ranging from alpine scrub vegetation in the higher reaches to sub-tropical moist evergreen forests down below, the vegetation of the region is varied. Sikkim Himalaya is richly endowed with biological resources spread over a variety of ecosystem types and a range of altitudes from the alpine rhododendron-dominated scrub forest through conifer forests with Abies densa and Tsuga domosa down to mixed evergreen forests, dominated by species such as Castonopsis spp., Qurecus lamellosa, Lithecarpus spicatus, Elaeocarpus lanceaefolius, Michilus edulis, and Michela spp. The region of Yuksam and Khecheopalri has all these species over a very short transect, running down from the alpine to the sub-tropical zone. Orchids are abundant, and there is rich wildlife of Himalayan black bear, musk deer, and fishing cat, leopard cat, red panda, black-capped langur and diverse bird life. Besides this, the area is also rich in valuable medicinal plants and herbs.

The soils of the area are highly variegated. The general soils of Sikkim are acidic in nature and are excessively drained with coarsely loamy to fine loamy in texture. The soil texture of the Yuksam-Dzongri Goechha La corridor is sandy loam and sandy, whereas the Khecheopalri Lake area is dominated by sandy loam texture. The very steep slopes (>50 %) represented by Typic Hapludolls and Dystic Eutrochrepts were largely under temperate forests. On the other hand, steep slopes (30-50%) with umbric Dystrochrepts and Cumulic Hapludolls experienced a thermic soil temperature regime. The steep slopes having a mesic soil temperature regime were represented by Entic Haplumbrepts and Typic Cryorthents. These were largely found under coniferous forests. The steep slopes of isofriged soil temperature regime were represented in general by shallow soils under alpine pasture (Das et al. 1998).

3.4. Cultural Setting

3.4.1. History

In 1975, Sikkim was merged as the 22nd state of India. The early history of Sikkim is mainly based on the Lepcha tradition. The history of the emergence of the kingdom of Sikkim can be traced back to the 17th century (Risley, 1968). Sikkim has a long tradition of the Buddhist religion. Since the rule of the Chogyal dynasty, when the first Chogyal (King) of Sikkim was crowned in 1642 in Norbugang in Yuksom, Buddhist traditions have become deeply ingrained into the psyche of the Sikkimese people (plate 1e). However, in proportional terms, Buddhism is practised by about 25% of the local population, while the majority religion is Hinduism (70%). However, Buddhism is evident in all walks of life, from rituals and festivals to tapestries richly woven with symbols from Buddhist myths and legends, to the typical Sikkimese architecture, and in the large number of monasteries and stupas dotting the landscape throughout the state. It is essential to note, however, that this unique culture, which has developed in Sikkim, represents a blend of the shared traditions of three communities: Buddhism among the Lepchas and Bhutias, and Hinduism among the majority Nepalese.

Of the four Buddhist sects, such as the Nyngmepa, Kagupa, Gelugpa and Sakyapa, represented in Sikkim, the Nyngmepa sect, initiated by the Buddha incarnate, Maha Guru Padmasambhava is the most significant. Sikkim, as a whole, is considered to be sacred by Sikkimese Buddhists. Padmasambhava, highly revered and worshipped by Sikkimese Buddhists, is considered to have blessed Yuksam and the surrounding landscape of Demojong, in the western part of Sikkim, by placing within it a large number of hidden treasures (ters). Many of the sacred treasures by Lhabstsun

Namkha Jigme in the Yuksam region are believed to be slowly revealed to enlightened lamas and discovered at appropriate times. Conserving and protecting these treasures from polluting and disturbing influences is considered vitally important for human welfare.

The area below Mount Khangchendzonga in the landscape of Demojong is the core of the sacred land of Sikkim. Yuksam is considered to be a 'Lakhang' (altar) and 'Mandala' where offerings are made to protective deities. Any major disruption in the landscape would disturb the ruling deities of the 109 hidden lakes along the Rathongchu River, thus leading to serious calamities. During a period of bloodshed in the past, for example, Lake Khecheopalari is thought to have moved away from the river. Many folklore and legends are associated with its formation and shape. As per the legend of the Sikkimese people, the lake looks like the footprint of Goddess Tara Jetsun Dolma.

3.4.2. Ethnic Groups, Distribution and Characteristics

Sikkim is rich in cultural diversity and has a multi-ethnic composition, comprising the Lepcha, Bhutia, Nepalese, and Limbu. The Lepchas are the original settlers of the state. A later arrival to this area includes the Bhutia from Tibet. The recent immigrants include Nepali ethnic groups in the nineteenth century and Tibetan refugees. From 1891 to the present day, the Nepali population has increased several times due to encouragement given to Nepali settlers in the first phase of the British protectorate (Rai, 1992).

The Lepchas are believed to be indigenous to Sikkim and known to Bonpo Shamanists. According to Lepcha tradition, they originated in Mayel, a legendary valley in the vicinity of Khangchendzonga, and have no tradition of migration (Gowloog, 1998). The Lepchas, who were known as Rong-pa or valley folk, were fairly widely distributed throughout Sikkim. Now, Lepchas generally sought assimilation into the Bhutia culture. Intermarriage between the two communities is common, and instances of Lepchas marrying Nepalese are not unusual, particularly amongst the Lepchas of the western part of Sikkim. Traditionally, Lepchas are hunters, food gatherers and prefer animal husbandry. Their economy is mainly based on land and forests. They have their own dress, food habits and festivals. The Lepcha women dress themselves in Gada, and the men dress themselves in Gyado. About 12% of the total population of the Yuksam area belongs to the

Lepcha community, whereas Khecheoplari Lake is mostly dominated by Lepchas (96%).

Bhutias in Sikkim are of Tibetan origin. They wear Tibetan-style clothes, and their language also has a Tibetan origin. The Bhutia women dress up in Bakkhu, a long double-breasted gown akin to a Japanese kimonos. This gown is fitted on the body with the Kelp of a cloth piece tied around the waist. Inside this gown, the women wear a loose blouse (hanju) with long sleeves. This dress is locally known as a Kho. Married women wear a lined apron (pangden), made of cloth, on the front from the waistcloth, often brocaded on both corners. The Bhutia men also wear Bakkhu with long sleeves. However, the use of trousers and a cap has become common. Intermarriage has become an increasingly frequent occurrence, particularly since the closure of Tibet. The Bhutias are Buddhists by religion and belong to the scheduled tribe. They constitute about 31% of the total population of Yuksam and 2% of the Khecheoplari Lake. The main festivals of this community are Sagadawa, Bum Chu rituals,

Pang Lhabsol and Losser. It is no wonder that the Rathongchu River is the focus of religious rituals. Bum Chu rituals are considered the holiest of all festivals, and are held annually at Tashiding monastery. Rathongchu River is said to turn white and start singing, and water is collected from the point where Rathongchu meets the Ringnyachu. It attracts thousands of devotees from around Sikkim and the neighbouring region. Other widespread rituals reflect the respect with which this region of sacred landscapes is worshipped and revered by its people. The generalized ritual practised during "Pang Lhabsol" to propitiate the various ruling deities of the mountain peak of the Khangchendzonga, the midland region of the Yuksam and the lowland down below, is carried out by Buddhists throughout Sikkim.

The Nepalese, who constitute the majority of the Sikkimese population, migrated from Nepal in the nineteenth century. They have retained a distinct cultural identity separate from the racial amalgam that had become Sikkimese. They dress differently and speak Nepali and Hindi. The Nepali women tie a cloth or Sari (gunyu) around their waist as a skirt with patuka and cover their torso with a blouse (cholo). The head is covered with a two-meter-long majetro, a kind of scarf. This dress is locally known as Fariya cholo or Gunyu cholo. Nepali men dress themselves up with a Dawra (shirt), Surwal (trousers), a coat and a Nepali cap. The study sites constitute about 17% of the total population of Yuksam and 2% of Khecheoplari

Lake. Desain is the biggest and most popular festival celebrated by the Hindu Nepalese. The other important festival is Tiwar (the festival of light). In this festival, the Goddess Laxmi is worshipped. In the evening on this day, women, both young and old, visit door to door singing Bhailo and accepting Bhaili, offering money. On the third day, brothers are blessed by the sisters, and male folk visit the door-to-door of the village community, singing Deoshirey.

3.4.3. Religion

Buddhism and Hinduism are the two main predominant religions of both the study sites. Besides these, there are Christians. The Lamaist Buddhist tradition and culture have left their indelible mark on Sikkimese life. The Lamaist tradition of worship still continues, and there are no fewer than 200 monasteries in Sikkim today. Prayer flags are seen fluttering everywhere, and turning the prayer wheels is still regarded as a step towards cleansing of the sins (plate 1f). The offering of "Khada" (a silken white and cream scarf) on any occasion signifies honour and respect and has become an integral part of Sikkimese culture today. The lakes throughout Sikkim hold great religious significance, and the Sikkimese of various races and religions deeply revere them.

3.4.4. Food Habits

Leaving aside a small fraction of the Hindu population, the Sikkimese are non-vegetarians, and beef eating is not uncommon. However, some Nepali Hindus take beef. Drinking liquor is quite common among all communities. Raksi and Chhang are the local brews prepared from rice and millet, respectively. Among the delicious food, Chhou-chhou, a Sikkimese parallel of Tibetan Chowmein, is relished by all communities. The other local foods are Gunduruk, Kenema, etc.

Despite its great heterogeneity, Sikkim maintains religious harmony and cultural coexistence. Festivals, irrespective of any ethnic group, are celebrated by all with great joy and enthusiasm. The state in itself presents a unique example of cultural amalgamation of all ethnic groups.

3.5. Institution and Infrastructure

Infrastructure facilities provide a strong base for the economic development of an area. A region with abundant resources will remain backwards unless its resources have suitable channels for exploitation. A good network of transport and communication, along with the provision of other services and amenities, at reasonable terms, would make the area more susceptible to economic development than one lacking in these facilities (Dobhal, 1987). This section deals with the existing institutional and infrastructure facilities in both sites.

3.5.1. Education

Regarding Sikkim, the overall literacy rate is generally not very poor in the state. According to the 1991 census, the percentage of literate persons was 56%, which is higher than the national average (52%). In the study sites, the literacy rate was 54% in the Yuksam area and 42% in the Khecheopalri area in 1997. Educational facilities in remote areas of the state are not sufficient. In Yuksam village, there were five primary schools (including one lower primary school) with 289 students and 15 teachers in 1997; the children from local households were reported to have attended school regularly. The Yuksam village has one secondary school (Table 3.1). Student enrollment from primary to secondary school is given in table 3.1. About 60% of the school-age population is actually enrolled. The drop-out rate is greater in higher classes. This is a serious issue, and the less educated population will continue to increase in the near future. The ratio of boys to girls students enrolled in Yuksalll is 49:51. Of the total number of students enrolled, 74% are in primary school, 22% are in middle school, and 4% are in high school. This suggests either a significant drop-out from primary to mid-level and high school or limited opportunities for higher education.

School attendance ranged from 40 to 50%. The most significant issue was the high rate of absenteeism among both teachers and students. In addition, the parents, most of whom are illiterate, do not encourage their children to attend school regularly. However, some parents send their children to attend school regularly, while others send their children to urban areas to receive a higher and better education. Non-formal and functional education is urgently needed in this area. There is a need to establish a higher secondary school with hostel facilities in the area.

The other site, Khecheopalri, has only one lower primary school with a total number of 25 students (Table 3.1). Villagers primarily depend on Pelling and Gyalshing for further education.

3.5.2. Health and Sanitation

The modern health facilities at both sites are extremely poor. A primary health centre (PHC) with a capacity of 10 beds in Yuksam has a scanty supply of medicine. It has two doctors with 6 supporting staff. The health care workers are often absent. The Khecheopalri Lake lacks this facility, and villagers are dependent on other areas. Thus, the local people are forced to rely upon traditional methods of treatment and the use of native herbs and medicinal plants. In general, people are not health-conscious and do not use preventive health measures. Basic hygiene is very poor in homes. The incidence of tuberculosis, stomach pain, anaemia, and leucorrhoea was found to be relatively high among the patients. This is mainly due to the poor diet and drinking habits of the people.

3.5.3. Trails and Roads

The terrain is hilly, rugged, and extremely difficult. The existing road network is far short of the needs of the region. The area is connected by a metalled road, which takes off from the National Highway No.31A near Melli and passes through Jorethang town of the south district and crosses the Rangit River to Nayabazar. From Nayabazar, the state highway proceeds northwards and ultimately reaches Gyalsingh via Legship town. From Namchi town of the south district and Singtam town of the east district, the state highway runs west, joins together and enters the west district at Legship, where it merges with the state highway coming up north from Jorethang. A state highway continues further northwards from Legship, reaches Tashiding and then extends up to Yuksam. A state highway also connects Khecheopalri Lake via Pelling. At present, most trekkers (70%) come here via Gangtok, and others through the Darjeeling town of West Bengal.

The physiographic structure determines the directions of the trail route mostly from north to south, along the river. Trekking in this area follows an age-old pattern of movement within the mountains. There are traditional migratory routes and seasonal encampments among highland pastures, which are used for grazing the animals and lead tourist expeditions into the remote areas. Among them, the important ones are mentioned here. The trekkers and HMI mountaineers usually start from Yuksam. The trail approaching Tshoka through Bakhim, passing through a steep slope, is very narrow (Plate 2a). From Bakhim to Tshoka, about 2 km of the trail is not in good condition and is especially dangerous for children and older trekkers. The trail width from Tshoka to Dzongri is wide, made of wooden planks in some places that serve as a path on the steep slope. Trekkers usually follow this trail. The HMI (Himalayan Mountaineering Institute) trainees follow the same route up to Tshoka. From Tshoka, they follow another route (Zamlingaon, Chaurithang, Bikbari and Chaurigang) to reach the base camp. It takes about four days. Another important trail in this site starts from Tashiding and follows the Labdong, Kasturioralo, Lampokhri route to reach Thangsing. This trail is not very popular, but a few trekkers have followed this trail in recent years.

The transportation facilities have improved now due to the flow of tourists in the area. Presently, the state transport department is plying two buses connecting Yuksam with Gyalshing and Jorethang. Besides this, the private taxis are also running between Yuksam and Gyalshing, Jorethang and Gangtok. The Khecheopalri Lake is also connected by bus services from Gyalshing.

3.5.4. Marketing

It is observed that both sites lack even the basic marketing facilities, both in terms of quantity and quality. The existence of merely 8 multipurpose shops, 5 grocery shops, 4 tea shops, 3 wine shops, 3 low-quality restaurants, and a few other miscellaneous shops characterizes Yuksam, while the Khecheopalri Lake has only two tea shops and one multipurpose shop. The needs of the people for medicines and other household items are fulfilled chiefly by the district headquarters at Gyalshing.

3.5.5. Communication

Communication facilities at both sites are very limited and not accessible to local people and trekkers (Table 3.1). The Yuksam area has only one sub-post office, whereas the people in the Khecheopalri area are dependent on this facility from nearby villages. The police checkpost at Yuksam has a wireless set and is connected to all police checkposts and the police headquarters at Gangtok. The Yuksam-Dzongri-Goechha La trek corridor is remote; therefore, improved communications along the trekking route are necessary. The establishment of wireless sets at various locations will help develop communications in this inaccessible area. Most importantly, a communication system with a wireless radio needs to be established in the

Yuksam-Dzongri-Goechala corridor, as well as another set at the Khecheopalri Lake site.

3.5.6. Institutional Framework

The Village Council is the main political organization at the village level, with the mandate to develop the village and make wise use of natural and cultural resources, and to promote income-generating activities. Each village council receives a nominal payment under the Jawahar Rozgar Yojna from the district as a grant to be used for development activities. Discussions with council members and community leaders revealed that they have a fair understanding of their villages, the surrounding areas, and the associated problems and potential development options. They seemed eager to take part in the planning, development and implementation of tourism projects. Besides the village council, local communities at both sites formed non-governmental organizations, namely the Khangchendzonga Conservation Committee (KCC) in the Yuksam area and the Khecheopalri Holly Lake Welfare Committee (KHLWC) in the Khecheopalri Lake site. The primary functions of these organizations are to raise awareness among villagers, schoolchildren, and visitors about the local environment and its conservation.

Yuksam is the last settlement in this trekking corridor, having a government guesthouse, a trekkers' hut, hotels/lodges, a police check post, a village council *bhawan*, and a wildlife interpretation centre. The tourism department has made trekkers' huts at Tshoka, Dzongri, Thansing and Samitti for trekkers in this trail route. Besides this, one forest guesthouse is available for tourists at Bakhim. In contrast, the other site, Khecheopalri Lake, lacks all these facilities, except for one trekkers' hut.

Parameters	Sites	
	Yuksam-Dzongri-Goechha La	Khecheopalri Lake
Educational Facilities		
Secondary School	1	--
Enrolled Students	456	--
Teacher student ratio	23	--
Primary & Lower primary school	7	1
Enrolled Students	361	25
Teacher students ratio	28	12
Health Facilities		
Primary Health Center (PHC)	1	--
Doctor	2	--
Other Staff	8	--
Animal Husbandry	1	--
Doctor	1	--
Other Staff	3	--
Transport and Communication		
Government Bus	2	1
Taxi services	5	--
Sub-post office	1	--
Telephone	1	--
Institutional Facilities		
Police Check Post	1	--
Village Council Bhawan	1	--
Wildlife Interpretation Center	1	--
Government guest house	3	--
Trekker's Hut	2	1
Hotel/Lodges	8	--

Table 3.1: Infrastructure Facilities Available at the Study Sites

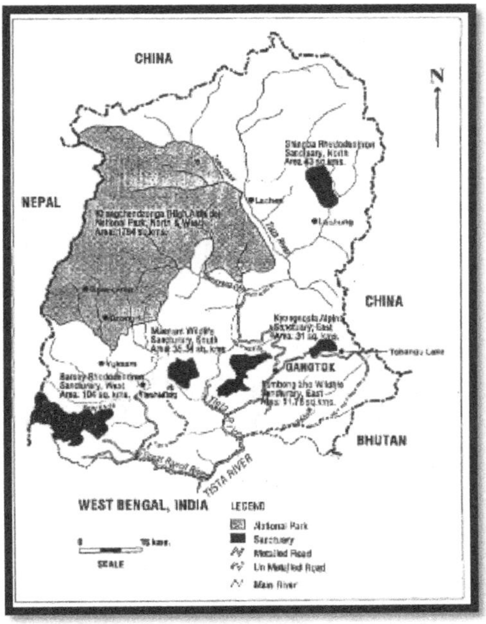

Figure 3.1: Map of Sikkim Showing Tourist Spots, National Park, Sanctuaries and Road Network

Figure 3.2: Location Map Showing the Yuksam-Dzongri-Goechha La Trekking Corridor of Khangchendzonga National Park and Sacred Khecheopalri Lake

Figure 3.3: Location of Holy Sites in Yuksam Area

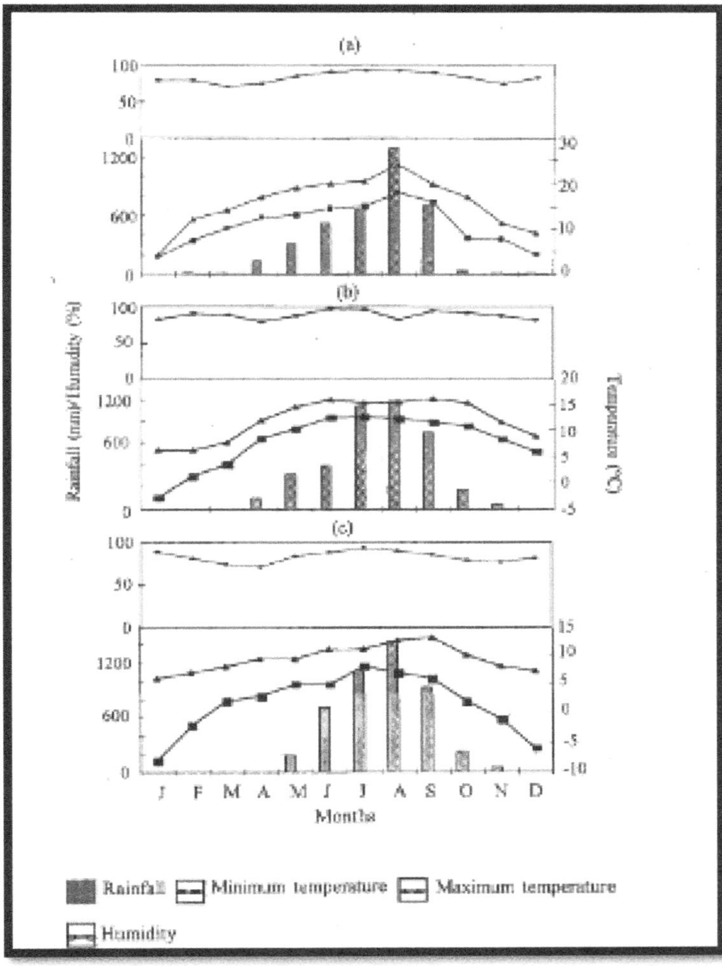

Figure 3.4: Temporal Variation of Temperature, Rainfall and Humidity at Three Major Halting Places (A = Yuksam, B = Tshoka, C = Dzongri).

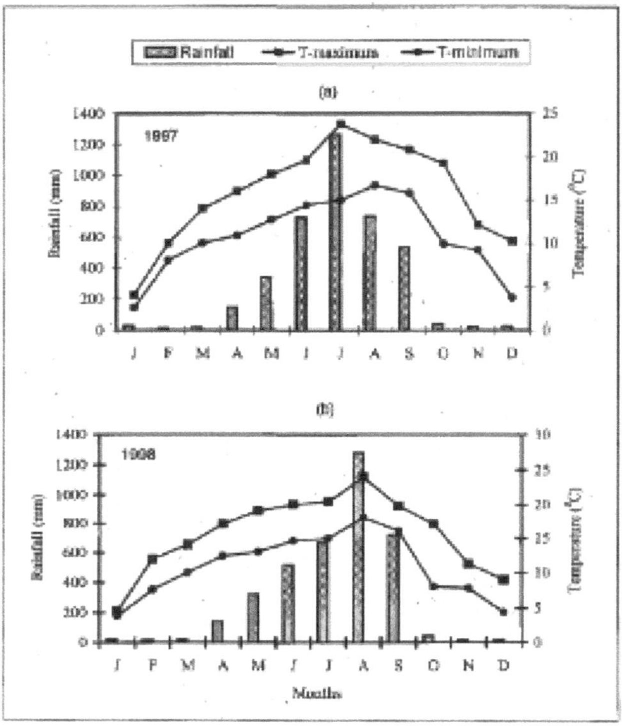

Figure 3.5: Temporal Distribution of Rainfall and Maximum and Minimum Temperature at the Khecheopalri Lak

Chapter 4 | Dynamics of Tourism

4.1. Introduction

Tourism is now one of the most rapidly expanding sectors within the world's largest and fastest-growing industry. It is emerging as a growing sector of economic development with an estimated annual growth rate of 10-15% (Sreedhar 1995a & b). Over the last two decades, the tourism sector has been a major growth sector and a significant source of employment (WTTC, 1995).

The magnificent, diverse landscapes and rich cultural heritage of Sikkim have attracted tourists, pilgrims, naturalists, explorers, trekkers, mountaineers and adventure travellers. Given the limited industrial growth in Sikkim, tourism can become a significant source of income generation in the remote mountain regions, thereby creating employment opportunities for local people. Over recent years, the area has undergone significant changes due to the growth of tourism. Since the 1990s, there has been a tremendous increase in the number of visitors, and its impact and implications in the area are enormous (Rai & Sundriyal, 1997). This chapter describes trekking/recreational travel, including its growth pattern, visitor demographics, age-sex structure, income and expenditure patterns, and market trend analysis related to tourism growth.

4.2. Methods

The scarcity of data has led to in-depth interviews and group discussions with practising professionals, visitors (including residents, non-residents, and FITS), local community leaders, and individuals directly involved in tourism-related activities. This section deals with both primary and secondary data sources. The primary data were collected through a structured questionnaire, with random sampling of 415 visitors in the Yukasam-Dzongri-Goechha La trekking corridor and 225 in the Khecheopalri Lake site, during 1997-98, using different types of questionnaires. The interviews were conducted over a period of six months (March to May and October to December), corresponding to two peak tourist seasons, and the assumptions of a representative sample are plausible. The samplings were done at different times of the day and on all days of the sample week to ensure a representative sample at both sites.

The main focus of the visitors' survey has been on preferences and behaviour patterns, as well as the attitude and overall reaction of visitors towards various aspects, including food, accommodation, transport, communication, recreation, and expenses on different items. The analysis of tourists' origin, their profession, income, purpose of visit, age-sex structure, and means of transport in the area used is helpful in reflecting the characteristics of tourists' behaviour, expenditure pattern and preferences. Besides visitors, tour operators were also interviewed to collect information on marketing and promotional materials used for better in-market and travel industry promotions. The survey was restricted to individuals involved in the industry and those who send visitors to trekking and the Lake site. This was to assess the problems faced by marketing and achieving targets with diverse partners around the world. The survey divided the tourism industry into the following sectors: tour operators, travel agents, hotels, tourism associations (TAAS), and the Department of Tourism, Government of Sikkim. Initially, it was intended to conduct a survey of all stakeholders; however, limited time and resources allowed for only 35 samples. Stakeholders were selected on the basis of activeness, and interviews were conducted only with senior and decision-making staff. The survey paid particular attention to tour operators because they are most closely involved in sending visitors to both sites. Before the interview, each operator was briefed on the purpose of the interview to avoid bias. The interview was conducted following a face-to-face interview and lasted between 30 and 40 minutes each.

In designing the questionnaire, the major concern has been to ensure that it does not produce predetermined results either by omitting unfavourable alternatives in multiple-choice questions or by suggesting desired responses through the phrasing and sequence of questions (Nixon, 1954). To avoid these problems, the adopted questionnaire comprised a series of alternative choice questions and ordering, which were arranged sequentially with a view to minimizing bias. However, it has been realized that it is not possible to eliminate all potential bias from a questionnaire. Formally, the questionnaire underwent a pre-test examination to identify potential weaknesses and add clarity and uniformity. This was accomplished by interviewing a few tourists/operators, and it was realized that some questions did not always lead to useful results. Therefore, in the final version of the questionnaire, the previous sets were removed and newer sets were added to the contents, aiming to reduce pace, time, and complexity on the one hand, while ensuring clear answers on the other.

The secondary data were generated from information on tourist inflow provided by the Tourism Department, Police Check Post (entry point), hotels/lodges, tour operators, and the Himalayan Mountaineering Institute (HMI) records.

4.3. Tourism Growth

The number of tourists visiting Sikkim has been growing at a very fast rate in recent years. The primary reason for this significant growth in tourist influx is the relaxation of regulations, which has opened up numerous new areas for both domestic and foreign visitors, as well as the development of tourist facilities in Sikkim as a whole in recent years. The real growth in the number of tourists in Sikkim began in 1980.

Until 1980, the state hosted only 10,000 visitors, which eventually increased to more than ten times that number in 1998. Since 1984, there has been a steady increase in the tourist flow. In 1989, approximately 46,416 visitors arrived in Sikkim, comprising 96% domestic and 4% foreign visitors. In contrast, in 1998, around 143,410 tourists visited Sikkim, with 93% being domestic and 7% foreign visitors. There was some indication of a decline in the number of visitors during 1986 and 1987 due to the Gorkha Land Movement in the adjoining Darjeeling hills of Sikkim (Figure 4.1). It is expected that by 2008, the number of visitors in Sikkim may reach up to 1,54,180, requiring a considerable increase in bed space capacity.

Tourism in the mountain region is a highly seasonal activity. The flow of visitors distinctly has two peaks annually, with a low profile from January to March and from July to September, and a high inflow from mid-March to June and from October to mid-December. During the spring and autumn seasons, the Sikkim Himalaya offers ideal conditions for recreation and trekking. The state hosts the majority of domestic visitors compared to foreign visitors. The majority of domestic visitors are from West Bengal (65%), followed by Delhi (10%), Bombay (6%), Madras (5%) and the remaining 14% from other parts of the country. The number of foreign visitors to Sikkim has also increased during recent years, comprising the following nationalities: UK (24%), USA (15%), Germany (13%), France

(10%), Japan (6%), Switzerland (5%), and the remaining 27% from other countries. More than 85% domestic and 65% foreign visitors visit for recreation, followed by 15% domestic and 35% foreigners who come exclusively for trekking. Out of the total visitors, about 42% of visitors have listed their primary motivation as trekking. This value does not include those visitors who merely do some trekking as part of a pleasure or culture-based trip. However, despite this steady increase, the reason for visits appears to have changed little over several years.

4.3.1. Purpose and Length of Visit

Concerning the purpose or reason for visiting the area, it is not easy to classify into groups because some visitors have more than a single purpose. Pleasure is the most important reason for a visit for both domestic and foreign visitors. At the second level, pilgrimage is the main cause to visit the Khecheopalri Lake, while trekking has been the main cause for visiting Yuksam-Dzongri-Goechha La corridor (Table 4.1). Among the pilgrimage activities, visits to the monasteries and offering rituals in the Khecheopalri Lake are the most important. Bird watching and wildlife viewing are other significant reasons for travel. It is evident from table 4.1 that most trekking travellers visit the site to enjoy the natural beauty and experience the wilderness.

The "total tourist-visitor-days" is a crucial factor for the host region, as it ultimately determines the total number of days tourists spend there, the requirements for hotel accommodations, catering facilities, and other related services. For visitors, the number of days spent travelling and the time allocated are important, as they aim to see as many places as possible within a limited duration. For domestic visitors, the average length of visit in Sikkim has been approximately 10 days, in which, on average, they spend 5 days in the trekking corridor. For foreign visitors, the average length of the entire journey is 15 days, with approximately 8 days spent trekking. In the case of Khecheopalri Lake, the majority (80%) of foreign visitors spend an average of 3 days at the site, and a few (20%) spend 3-5 days viewing the surrounding area.

4.3.2. Pattern of Trekking

The Yuksam-Dzongri-Goechha La corridor inside the Khangchendzonga National Park (KNP), recently designated as a biosphere reserve, is the most popular trekking destination in Sikkim. Trekking travel on this trail started in 1960. A Kalimpong-based tour operator, according to local people, organized the first trek in 1973. Sikkim State opened its borders to foreigners in 1980. The rise of Sikkim's popularity as an adventure travel destination began in 1990. The period 1992-97 showed a steady rise in the number of tourists who entered Sikkim for trekking purposes (Figure 4.2). In 1997, about 2002 visitors came exclusively to trek in the high mountains. The Himalayan Mountaineering Institute (HMI) also conducts eight training courses, consisting of 1,379 trainees. The trail is crowded, particularly during the summer and fall seasons (Table 4.2). Foreign visitors require an entry permit to visit Sikkim, as well as a trekking permit for a maximum duration of 15 days. Foreign visitors are allowed to go on treks only in groups of at least 4 persons. Tour operators arrange the visit and charge daily rates, including food and guides, at rates ranging from US$25 to US$50 per person per day. Alternatively, domestic visitors may trek without a group. In the latter case, economic benefits may be dispersed more widely among the local people. But the primary source of tourist-related income is from guided treks. Thus, a huge amount of foreign visitors' investment goes to travel agents.

Since ancient times, the people of Sikkim have visited the Khecheopalri Lake for pilgrimage purposes. Tourists started coming to this lake after 1980 (according to local people), and the number has started to increase at a high rate since 1990. The data on tourist flows to this site are not properly recorded and maintained. The magnitude of tourist flows may testify to the increasing economic importance of tourism, but on the other hand, its impact on the lake ecosystem seems serious. The number of visitors has grown rapidly from 16068 in 1997 to 18713 in 1998 (Figure 4.3). Approximately 55% were domestic, followed by 42% Sikkimese pilgrims and 3% foreign visitors. The visit to the Khecheopalri Lake is distributed throughout the year. According to local people and observations made during the survey, the months of April and October are relatively representative of the overall mix of visitors. The majority of domestic visitors come from the state of West Bengal in India, while most foreign visitors are free and independent trekkers (FITs).

4.3.3. Age-Sex Structure of Visitors

Analysis of the age structure of tourists who arrived indicates that the middle-aged group (21-60 years) holds a dominant position at both sites. It is observed from table 4.3 that tourists below the age of 20 years constitute only 1%, while the age group of 60 years and above has also been estimated at 1% each. The percentage of male visitors has been higher than that of females for both domestic and foreign visitors, mainly due to difficult terrain and inaccessibility.

4.3.4. Educational Level and Profession of the Visitors

In terms of the educational qualification of visitors, the majority of both domestic and foreign visitors are bachelor's degree holders. A small fraction of domestic and foreign visitors has an educational qualification at the graduation level (Table 4.4). This suggests that educational qualification does not significantly influence trekking travel motivation.

In reference to profession-wise distribution of domestic and foreign visitors, executives (government sector) recorded the highest percentage, followed by students, businessmen and retired personnel at both the sites (Table 4.5).

4.3.5. Mode of Travel

It is evident from table 4.6 that the principal mode of travel to the sites by both domestic and foreign visitors is a reserved taxi, followed by a shared taxi, and lastly by government-run buses. For non-resident visitors, the tour operator organizes taxis, while the resident visitors arrange themselves. The FITs generally prefer government-run buses and single-seat shared taxis.

4.3.6. Type of Accommodation Availed

During the survey, it was observed that the majority of domestic and foreign visitors took accommodation in tourist huts, followed by hotels/lodges. However, this changed in 1998, primarily due to the construction of a 3-star hotel at Yuksam. Presently, more than 50% of the domestic and foreign visitors are staying in hotels at Yuksam. Except for one, the other hotels are lower-budget hotels that offer simple accommodation. All budget lodges need to improve their toilets, bathing facilities, and housekeeping. However, at the Khecheopalri Lake site, the majority of visitors (both domestic and foreign) stays in tourist huts as hotel facilities are not available. A very small number of foreign visitors and Sikkimese pilgrims prefer to stay in monasteries (Table 4.7). About 40% of the domestic visitors prefer to stay at Pelling. Huts at Yuksam, on the trekking route and the Khecheopalri Lake, are not in an appealing condition for trekkers seeking quality service. Huts need to have basic cleanliness, including clean and working toilets and bathrooms, clean sheets and blankets, and a clean kitchen.

4.3.7. Income Structure and Expenditure Pattern

The per capita daily spending of tourists is a significant factor with economic implications. As mentioned earlier, it is influenced by the income of tourists and the relative prices of different classes of products/services they purchase while travelling. The majority of the domestic visitors belong to the lower-middle (Rs. 2000 to Rs. 6000) and middle class (Rs. 6000 to Rs. 10000) income groups. In the case of foreign visitors, they belong to the middle and upper middle class (Rs. 10000 to Rs. 20000) (Table 4.8). During personal conversations, a large number of foreign visitors expressed that visiting India is cheaper than visiting most other countries. A positive correlation was observed between the duration of stay and spending capacity, indicating that high-income group tourists stay longer and spend more at the sites compared to relatively low-income group tourists. The major source of tourist-related income is from organized treks. Although the trainees of the Himalayan Mountaineering Institute (HMI) are small in number, they are a significant contributor to the overall picture of tourists' activity in the trekking corridor. They frequently employ hundreds of pack animal porters to carry their goods and equipment from Yuksam to base camp, and add a significant amount to the local economy.

The tourist-cum-pilgrims from Sikkim visit the Khecheopalri Lake more frequently than the tourists from distant areas. The expenditure pattern has been classified into 4 main groups, that is:

- Boarding and lodging, including entertainment,
- Internal transport,
- Shopping, and
- Miscellaneous

In fact, the expenditure pattern is one of the most important parameters in the surveys of tourist traffic, on account of the multiplying economic benefits derived from the foreign exchange brought in by the foreign tourists and spent by them. The average per capita expenditure incurred by both domestic and foreign visitors ranges from US$5 to US$45, depending on the nature of income and type of trek. Food and lodging are the most important items of expenditure. The expenditure on this item is slightly higher in the case of foreign visitors than their counterparts at both sites. Shopping for both types of visitors is placed in second position. Most of the FITs spend very little compared to those who come through an organized trek. However, their expenditure directly benefits the local community.

4.3.8. Visitors' Opinions and Reactions

About the opinion of the "food', the majority of the domestic and foreign visitors consider it as "Good" in quality as well as in taste, whereas the lack of good restaurants at both sites has also been noted. When asked about the accommodation facility, most of the visitors stated that it is just about "Average". The trekker huts are over-crowded during peak tourist season, and camping at sites is generally observed (Plate 2b).

The general opinion of visitors about the local people from both sites is very satisfactory. Both domestic and foreign visitors consider local people as "hospitable, charming, cheerful and very religious" (Table 4.9 & 4.10). Very few domestic visitors contact the government-run Tourist Information Centre at Gangtok; on the other hand, most of the foreign FITs receive information from the Tourist Information Centre at Gangtok. Overall, the visitors are satisfied with the assistance and facilities provided by the tourist information centre as well as tour operators.

A considerable number of the visitors strongly express their discontent with the condition of the trail. Most of the domestic and foreign visitors frequently mention the litter along the trail and at the campsite. In general, most of the visitors express their satisfaction with the local hospitality and food. However, a few visitors are disappointed during their stay in the trekker's huts. As a whole, the majority of the domestic and foreign visitors are satisfied with the site's appearance. However, for a sustained rate of growth of the tourist industry, the complaints deserve urgent attention and remedial measures.

4.4. Tourism Marketing

Sikkim lacks visibility in the market compared to other Himalayan destinations, such as Nepal, Bhutan, Ladakh, and Tibet. In addition, there is a general vague notion in the market that Sikkim is difficult to get into and that permits are difficult to obtain. There is very little coverage of Sikkim in the press media. There is limited awareness about Sikkim among the general travel public in India, except for those in West Bengal. Internationally, there is virtually no awareness of Sikkim as an ecotourism adventure travel destination compared to other Himalayan adventure destinations. There is little or no television coverage because of permit restrictions. This section discusses approaches that should be taken to regulate tourism by operators and institutions involved with sending visitors to the trail and the Lake site.

4.4.1. Marketing Products

Sikkim's most conspicuous attraction is its excellent biodiversity. This is what sets Sikkim aside from other Himalayan destinations. In addition, the Sikkim Kargu and Ningmapa monasteries, located at the study sites, have an ancient history, and their art has largely been well-preserved in several of these monasteries. The monastic culture is well-preserved and has not been well-exposed to the international market. The high-altitude areas, especially the Khangchendzonga (the third-highest mountain in the world) base camp area and sacred lakes, offer a great tourism product. The Yuksam-Dzongri-Goechala La trekking corridor is the only high-altitude trek route open to serious trekkers in Sikkim. During the spring/summer and autumn trek season, the agency-based and private treks are operated by both TAAS and non-TAAS members. HMI operates its mountaineering training programs. There are also non-trekking domestic visitors who come to Yuksam and its environs. There are a few visitors to Yuksam in the winter months, too. A trek day is operated on similar lines to those in Nepal. Breakfast is typically Western, and packed lunches and hot dinners are served, with menus featuring a variety of Western, Indian, and Sikkimese items. Tour operators are most active with value-adding practices such as providing information about destinations (Table 4.1). Before the adventure and trek products can be promoted in particular, Sikkim needs to be promoted as a destination with its unique selling points, both in India and the international market. At the same time, in order to attract and satisfy/maintain quality clients, certain products have to be developed. Currently, one/two agents are selling a diversified range of trek products in Nepal, Bhutan, and Tibet, offering a year-round selection of products. The Sikkim trek product has a fairly short season in the spring and summer, as well as in autumn, which can be diversified to offer year-round attractions.

4.4.2. Promotional Materials

The maintenance and promotion of natural, social, and cultural diversity are essential for long-term, sustainable tourism, creating a resilient base for the industry. In most of the areas, there is a lack of tourism promotion in general and trekking in particular. The lack of promotional measures in Sikkim is a significant hindrance to selling its products. Currently, the promotional activities of Sikkim-based tour operators are being advertised only in Indian newspapers and magazines, targeting direct walk-in clients. A few operators with proven service are handling referral business from Nepal, and a few operators are handling business from foreign individual motivators and agents. Some operators have established an email, and one operator has a website.

TAAS and some operators have developed promotional brochures. These brochures are used for marketing purposes, but only 3 or 4 operators have acceptable quality materials suitable for the international market (Table 4.12). The tourism department's brochure is primarily aimed at the domestic market, featuring package tour information, as well as two additional brochures covering destination information and adventure/trek options. A high-quality brochure is crucial for effective tourism marketing.

4.4.3. Economic Worth of the Tourism Industry

The price of the products offered by tour operators varies between operators and the quality of the products. About 15 TAAS agents are actively operating treks on the Yuksam-Dzongri-Goechha La route with 303 pax (persons) and non-TAAS members with 591 pax as observed in 1997. A few agents also operate short treks or walks on the Pemayangtse/Khecheopalri/Yuksam/Tashiding route. The trek price for foreign visitors ranges from US$25 to US$50 per person per day, depending on the group size and services provided. Sometimes, the trek price is as low as US$15 per person per day, as has also been quoted in competitive situations or for walk-in clients, where the service level is probably sacrificed. Agents who are more aware of the trek market in Nepal and other parts of India have quoted between US$35 and US$60 per pax per day to position the product more realistically in terms of competitive trek products in Nepal. But there are also low-quality treks being operated by some agents who undertake treks for clients at a given price. The trek price is low for domestic visitors, ranging from US$15 to US$35 per person per day, depending on the quality of service. Most of the income generated by tour operators is from guided treks. Assessing the economic value of the tour operators is a complex task. The estimated total turnover from tourism was Rs 11728289 (US$286,080) in 1998 (Table 4.13). An additional income is also generated from the sale of local crafts to the visitors. Approximately 13 agents allocate between 10% and 25% of their profit or income revenue to marketing activities.

4.5. Conclusion

Sikkim is endowed with a wealth of natural and cultural attractions, and it does not require significant investment in hotel construction. As a matter of fact, these would scar the landscape of Sikkim. Adventure/trekking travel is growing rapidly, and there is a need to link this growth with environmental awareness among both visitors and the host community. This is crucial for maintaining cultural traditions, as the benefits derived from tourism should serve as incentives to promote conservation practices and mitigate environmental degradation. A travel agent plays a key role in the development of the travel industry, with wide coverage in television, as well as in the press and consumer magazines. For effective marketing, tour operators should attend key travel fairs in Asia and Europe to establish connections with foreign agents and generate future business. Time-to-time press releases on the travel industry, events, festivals and any new area opening should be sent to travel trade publications and other media. Agent fame trips are the best way to get an agent to see the product first-hand and meet with ground operators. Once an agent is excited about the destination and enjoys its people's hospitality, there is a good chance they will sell the destination.

Values in Parentheses Are Percentages

Purpose	Yuksam-Dzongri-Goechha La Corridor				Khecheopalri Lake			
	Domestic		Foreign		Domestic		Foreign	
	No	%	No	%	No	%	No	%
Holiday/Pleasure	36	20.34	73	30.67	96	61.94	73	73.00
Trekking/ Mountaineering	123	69.49	155	65.13	3	1.94	19	19.00
Religious/pilgrimage	10	5.65	7	2.94	56	36.12	6	6.00
Others	8	4.52	3	1.26	-	-	2	2.00
Total	177	100.00	238	100.00	155	100.00	100	100.00

Table 4.1: Distribution of Tourists Classed on the Purpose of the Visit at the Study Sites, 1997-1998

Seasons	Yuksam-Dzongri-Goechha La Corridor						Khecheopalri Lake					
	Domestic		Foreign		HMI		Domestic		Foreign		Local Pilgrims	
	Individual	Groups	Individual	Groups	Individual	Groups	individual	Groups	Individual	Groups	Individual	Groups
Winter	6 (0.94)	2	18 (2.72)	7	315 (22.84)	5	685 (8.65)	98	74 (14.37)	25	178 (3.45)	18
Spring	35 (5.45)	7	146 (22.05)	30	342 (24.80)	5	1900 (23.94)	271	198 (38.45)	66	3440 (66.85)	344
Summer	287 (44.70)	37	145 (21.90)	37	351 (25.45)	6	2253 (28.38)	322	118 (22.92)	39	763 (14.83)	76
Rainy	31 (4.83)	8	26 (3.93)	6	181 (13.13)	4	558 (7.03)	80	37 (7.18)	12	252 (4.89)	25
Fall	283 (44.08)	50	327 (49.40)	52	190 (13.78)	2	2540 (32.00)	363	88 (17.08)	29	514 (9.98)	51
Total	642	104	662	132	1379	22	7936	1134	515	171	5147	514

Table 4.2: Seasonal Variation in Visitors Inflow to the Study Sites, 1997-1998

Age-group	Yuksam-Dzongri-Goechha La Corridor								Khecheopalri Lake							
	Domestic				Foreign				Domestic				Foreign			
	Male		Female		Male		Female		Male		Female		Male		Female	
	No	%	No	%	No	%	No	%	No	%	No	%	No	%	No	%
Below 20	3	1.69	1	0.56	5	2.10	3	1.26	6	3.87	2	1.29	2	2.00	2	2.00
21 – 40	96	54.24	30	16.95	83	34.87	57	23.95	71	45.81	38	24.52	29	29.00	22	22.00
41 – 60	47	26.55	-	-	59	24.79	20	8.40	20	12.90	13	8.38	21	21.00	19	19.00
Above 60	-	-	-	-	8	3.36	3	1.26	2	1.29	3	1.94	4	4.00	1	1.00
Total	146	82.49	31	17.51	155	65.13	83	34.87	99	63.87	56	36.13	56	56.00	44	44.00

Table 4.3: Distribution of Tourists by Age and Sex Categories in the Study Sites, 1997-1998

Education level	Yuksam-Dzongri-Goechha La Corridor				Khecheopalri Lake			
	Domestic		Foreign		Domestic		Foreign	
	Number	%	Number	%	Number	%	Number	%
Upto Senior Secondary	35	19.77	38	15.97	69	45.52	18	18.00
Bachelor Degree	110	62.15	140	58.82	75	48.39	63	63.00
Master Degree	22	12.43	49	20.59	5	3.23	8	8.00
Other	10	5.65	11	4.62	6	3.87	11	11.00
Total	177	100.00	238	100.00	155	100.00	100	100.00

Table 4.4: Classification of Tourists on Educational Qualification, 1997-1998

Profession	Yuksam-Dzongri-Goechha La Corridor				Khecheopalri Lake			
	Domestic		Foreign		Domestic		Foreign	
	No.	%	No.	%	No.	%	No.	%
Govt. Service	99	55.93	96	40.34	93	60.00	38	38.00
Professional / Private Sector	25	14.12	120	50.42	12	7.74	46	46.00
Business	16	9.04	9	3.78	8	5.16	7	7.00
Students	37	20.90	8	3.36	6	3.87	6	6.00
Retired persons	-	-	5	2.10	7	4.52	3	3.00
Others	-	-	-	-	29	18.71	-	-
Total	177	100.00	238	100.00	155	100.00	100	100.00

Table 4.5: Profession-Wise Distribution of Tourists Visiting the Study Sites, 1997-1998

Mode of travel	Yuksam-Dzongri-Goechha La Corridor				Khecheopalri Lake			
	Domestic		Foreign		Domestic		Foreign	
	No	%	No	%	No	%	No	%
SNT (Bus)	17	9.60	26	10.92	30	19.35	75	75.00
Private Bus	31	17.51	37	15.55	-	-	-	-
Reserved Taxi	28	15.82	150	63.03	115	74.19	10	10.00
Shared Taxi	101	57.06	25	10.50	10	6.45	15	15.00
Total	177	100.00	238	100.00	155	100.00	100	100.00

SNT=Sikkim Nationalized Transport

Table 4.6: Mode of Travel of Visitors to the Study Sites, 1997-1998

Accommodation availed	Yuksam-Dzongri-Goechha La trekking corridor				Khecheopalri Lake			
	Domestic		Foreign		Domestic		Foreign	
	No	%	No	%	No	%	No	%
Hotel/lodges	54	30.51	116	48.74	114	73.55	-	-
Trekker's hut	116	65.54	60	25.10	7	4.51	93	93.00
Tent	7	3.95	62	26.05	-	-	-	-
Monastery	-	-	-	-	19	12.26	7	7.00
Others	-	-	-	-	15	9.68	-	-
Total	177	100.00	238	100.00	155	100.00	100	100.00

Table 4.7: Distribution of Tourists According to the Types of Accommodation Availed, 1997-1998

Income level category*	Yuksam-Dzongri-Goecha La trekking corridor		Khecheopalri Lake	
	Domestic	Foreign	Domestic	Foreign
Less than Rs 2000	13.65	-	15.82	-
Rs 2001-6000	56.70	-	59.33	-
Rs 6001-10000	27.18	0.84	22.00	1.14
Rs 10001-20000	2.47	7.45	2.85	9.30
Above Rs 20000	-	91.71	-	89.56

*Income per month

Table 4.8: Percent of Income Level Categories of Tourists Visiting the Study Sites, 1997-1998

Visitors' Opinion	Likert-scale				
	Very Good	Good	Poor	Very Poor	No opinion
Local people's hospitality	64	27	7	-	2
Quality of local food	19	63	14	1	3
Accommodation at Camp site	7	67	12	8	6
Scenery	78	22	-	-	-
Wildlife sightings	-	2	36	40	22
Environmental awareness of staff	25	49	13	10	3
Litter at Camp-site & along the trail	17	23	51	9	-
Condition of the trail	-	11	60	29	-
Condition of the corridor forest	25	46	19	10	-

Table 4.9. Opinion of Visitors (%) on Yuksam-Dzongri-Goechha La Corridor, 1997-1998

Visitors' Opinion	Likert-scale				
	Very Good	Good	Poor	Very Poor	No opinion
Local people's hospitality	78	20	-	-	2
Quality of local food	60	22	7	-	11
Accommodation at lake site	36	55	7	-	2
Scenery	74	26	-	-	-
Litter in the lake surrounding area	11	34	25	20	10
Condition of the lake	15	30	24	10	21
Condition of the lake surrounding forest	16	61	6	7	10

Table 4.10: Opinion of Visitors (%) on the Khecheopalri Lake, 1997-1998

Products	Tour Operators	
	Number	%
Trekking	6	17
Cultural/Religious Tours	3	9
Mountaineering Expedition	1	3
Bird watching/Butterfly	1	3
Rafting/Water sports	2	6
Rhododendron/Orchid trek	2	6
Package tour/ sight scene	20	56

Table 4.11: Types of Tourism Products Offered by the Tour Operators to the Visitors, 1997-1998

Promotional measures	Tour operators	
	Number	%
Website	6	17
National News Paper	5	14
Travel Magazine	8	23
Tourism/Trade Fair & Conference	5	14
T. V. Channel (Local)	4	11
Sign Board/Banner	7	21

Table 4.12: Promotional Measures Used by Tour Operators, 1997-1998

Years	Revenue (US$)		
	TAAS members	Non-TAAS members	Total
1996	72240	159320	231560
1997	78968	172976	251944
1998	96960	189120	286080

Table 4.13: Revenue Received by TAAS and Non-TAAS Members from Tourists Visiting Sikkim

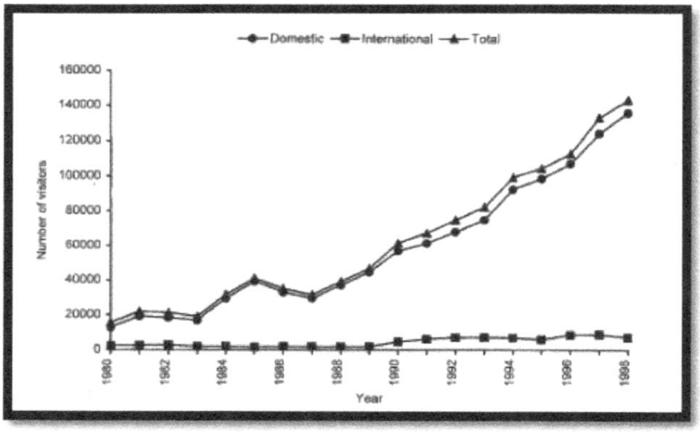

Figure 4.1: Yearly Visitor Profile from 1980 to 1998 in Sikkim

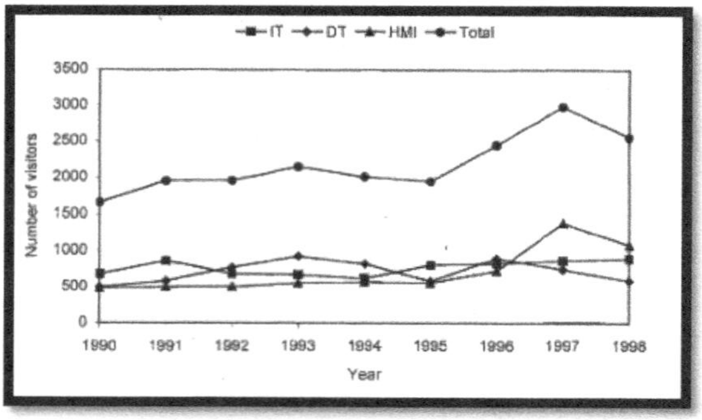

Figure 4.2: Annual Flow of Visitors to the Yuksam-Dzongri-Goechha La Trekking Corridor (IT=International Tourist, DT=Domestic Tourist, HMI=Himalayan Mountaineering Institute)

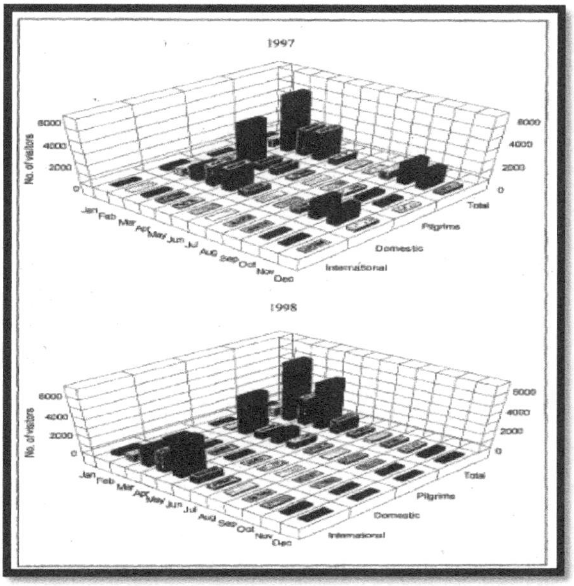

Figure 4.3: Visitors Flow in the Khecheopalri Lake during 1997 and 1998

Chapter 5| Socio-economic Development

5.1. Introduction

The livelihood in Sikkim is at the subsistence level, with three major options: traditional farming, pastoralism, and tourism. The major livelihood of the Sikkimese people is farming (Jana, 1994). Pastoralism is mainly concentrated in the high-altitude pasturelands, which are primarily used for grazing. Yaks/Dzos are reared for various purposes such as wool, meat, milk and milk-derived items like churpi and also as pack animals. Tourism has been one of the major economic activities in Sikkim for the past decade (Sharma, 1997). The local communities involved in tourism-related activities include lodge operators, porters, pack animal porters and teashops. The major economic changes that took place after 1990 have altered not only the economic landscape of the area but also many aspects of its social life. The changes in food consumption resulting from economic changes have also received some attention. Therefore, this chapter discusses the socio-economic characteristics, economic development indicators, inventory of physical assets, and quality of life, among others.

5.2. Methods

Socio-economic baseline information collected employs qualitative and quantitative procedures and sampling techniques that are widely accepted and scientifically sound, including group and individual questionnaire interviews, focused topic interviews and meetings, as well as semi-structured and open-ended interviews on various aspects of the household economy, such as the demographic features, occupational structure, literacy, cropping pattern, consumption pattern, and so on. While analyzing the livelihood options, the socio-economic aspects of the different stakeholders were considered important factors, along with the physical and institutional infrastructure that shape the nature of the livelihood options being practised by the stakeholders. Thereafter, the impact of livelihood options was analyzed in terms of their effects on the quality of life and equity.

The data used for consumption patterns are from National Food Balance Sheets based on agricultural production. For over one hundred different foods, the total weight of domestic production in a year is added to imports and any amounts withdrawn from stock. From this total are deducted exports, the amount used for seed and for feed, and those crops destined for other uses. An arbitrary 10% is subtracted for wastage between the farm gate and the real outlet. This final figure is then converted into calories per capita per day, grams of protein per capita per day and grams of fat per capita per day (FAO, 1991 & 1994). The food balance sheet has drawbacks; it is not a measure of consumption but an estimate of the amount of food available at the retail level. Consumption at the household level is lower than that in the food balance sheets that constitute the national average (Dowler & Seo, 1985 and Smil, 1987). The accuracy of the final estimates of food availability is dependent on the reliability of the production. The utilization of crops for seed and feed is not exactly known even in the developed countries (Grigg, 1996). Further, a substantial proportion of food is consumed on the farm and not recorded in survey statistics. However, there are only comprehensive international statistics on food availability, and they accurately represent major differences in consumption.

5.3. Socio-economic Characteristics

The total population of Yuksam and Khecheopalri villages was 988 and 463 in 1971, which rose to 1,930 and 797 in 1991. At the time of the survey (1997), the population reached 2622 and 958, respectively. The growth rate was thus estimated to be 45% and 27% within a decade (1981-1991).

The working population in the age group of 20 to 60 years is significantly higher at both the sites (Table 5. l). The percentage of school-going children is higher in the sacred Khecheopalri Lake site than in the Yuksam-Dzongri-Geochha La corridor. The sex ratio in the state still remains significantly lower than the national average of 927 and also lower than that of the other Himalayan states, except for Arunachal Pradesh (Sharma & Sharma, 1997). In contrast to this, the number of females per thousand males is higher (972) in the Yuksam-Dzongri-Goechha La corridor than the Sikkim and national average.

The population density has increased significantly over the last two decades, from 30 km2 in 1971 to 57 km2 in 1991, in the state. However, taking into account the fact that nearly 25% of the total geographical area of the state is uninhabited, the density of population in the Yuksam-Dzongri-

Geochha La corridor and sacred Khecheopalri Lake is slightly higher than the state average. However, another way of gauging the population pressure on land is the density of population km2 of arable land. The density of population km2 of arable land comes to as high as 595 and 260 persons, indicating a high pressure on arable land.

About 69% of the total households are involved in tourism. Out of that, 5% are engaged in hotel/lodges, 14% are pack-animal operators, 66% are porters, 9% own fair price shops and 6% own tea stalls. In the Khecheopalri area, only 3% of the total population is involved in tourism-related activities, and the rest belongs to the non-tourism sector.

5.3.1. Level of Education

The extent of human resource development in terms of literacy is significantly higher in the Yuksam-Dzongri-Geochha La corridor than in the Sacred Khecheopalri Lake (Table 5.2). The female literacy rates (43% and 47%) are lower than the male rates (53% and 57%) at both sites. Stakeholder-wise, the highest literacy rate was recorded in tourism-involved households and the lowest in non-tourism-involved households (Table 5.2). These differences can be attributed, in part, to the involvement of Bhutias in the tourism sector, which had remained the privileged ruling community and enjoyed state patronage until the state's merger with India in 1975. Secondly, the tourism industry enables families to earn more cash income, allowing them to afford higher and better education outside their area and state. Between tourism- and non-tourism-involved families, the percentage of the illiterate population is higher in non-tourism-involved families at both sites.

5.3.2. Land Utilization and Agricultural Production

The survey revealed the following land-use categories in Yuksam and Khecheopalri villages. The total area of Yuksam and Khecheopalri villages is 1244 ha and 987 ha, respectively. Out of that 35% and 37% are under net sown area, 28% and 12% are under fallow, 8% and 5% are under other cultivable land, excluding fallow, and 3% and 6% are under area not available for cultivation, respectively (Figure 5.1). The per capita land is 0.28 and 0.32 ha in Yuksam and Khecheopalri villages, respectively, which is quite low compared to other Himalayan regions. Nearly 35% and 50% of the total operational landholdings are of small size (1-2 ha) in Yuksam and Khecheopalri villages, respectively.

Table 5.3 shows the cropping pattern of both the villages. A large cardamom (Amomum subulatum)-based agroforestry system accounted for approximately 47% and 53% in Yuksam and Khecheopalri villages, respectively. Other important crops are maize (Zea mays) and potatoes (Solanum tuberosum), which accounted for more than 27% and 37%, respectively, in Yuksam and Khecheopalri villages. For the last 10 to 15 years, large cardamom farming has increased rapidly in both the villages. Farmers in Yuksam village have converted their paddy fields to large cardamom fields to generate more revenue. Among different categories of farmers, small-holding (1-2 ha) farmers have devoted more land to maize and potatoes than the large-holding (above ha) farmers, who have devoted more land to large cardamom cultivation.

The primary source of employment and income was overwhelmingly agriculture until 1996, with 80% of the total population engaged in subsistence farming. There has been a minor change in this situation in recent years. Despite this activity, it is doubtful whether subsistence-level nutritional requirements are met by local production. World Bank (1976) estimates that nutritional needs for normal subsistence should provide an average of 11.3 MJ adult-I day-I (9.2 MJ for minimum subsistence). Estimates show that the average nutrient intake actually available to the people of the Yuksam and Khecheopalri area is 2 MJ per person per day, which indeed appears to be far below the World Bank estimates (Table 5.3). These low values are calculated based solely on the local production system, and they clearly indicate that at both sites, people are more dependent on outside supplies to meet their daily nutritional needs. When compared to other similar studies in the Nepal Himalayan region, the nutrient intake was 5 MJ per person per day (Mahat et al., 1987), which is significantly higher than that in the present study. However, this indicates that the mountain region is one of the food-deficient areas, and the figures are not significantly different.

5.3.3. Livestock Holding

The livestock numbers of both sites are presented in table 6.6. It shows that cattle, goats, pigs, sheep and poultry birds are important animals. A total of 1,557 livestock have been recorded at Yuksam, while only 304 have been recorded at Khecheopalri. The animals include cattle (26%), goat (18%), sheep (27%), dzo (7%), yak (5%), horse (2%) and pigs (15%) in Yuksam area and cattle (36%), goat (35%), sheep (7%) and pig (22%) in the Khecheopalri Lake area. Almost all households keep poultry birds, which, besides enriching their diet, also enable them to meet emergency cash requirements. The cattle reared are mostly local breeds, which yield less milk. There is a significant difference in the number of animals owned by different stakeholders in both sites (Table 5.4). A highly significant difference is observed in the case of pack animal operators who rear a large number of Yak/Dzo for tourism purposes. Non-tourism-involved families also have large numbers of livestock because their economy is based on animal populations.

5.4. Indicators on Economic Development

The role of tourism in local, state and national economic restructuring has been widely stressed (HMSO, 1985; Grolleau, 1988). Local communities at both sites have recently reoriented their local economies and lifestyles around tourism. Until 1996, more than 50% of all community households had income from the agriculture sector only. Since then, involvement in tourism has risen in most villages, and it has become increasingly common for several members of a household to have tourism-based incomes. For most families, tourism earnings come from employment in trekking as guides, pack animal operators and cooks. Some men work exclusively for mountaineering as pack animal operators.

Employment in both trekking and mountaineering is seasonal. Hotels/lodges have become an increasingly important part of both the local and state economies. Most lodges are operated by women of the household, who typically employ one or two non-family persons to help with cooking, water heating, and cleaning.

5.4.1. Income

The people of Yuksam and the Khecheopalri Lake area have reoriented their local economy around tourism. In 1997, approximately 46% and 7% of the total household income came from this source in Yuksam and Khecheopalri, respectively. However, involvement in tourism-related activities has increased to 69% and 22% at these sites in 1998, and it has become increasingly common for local communities to be involved in tourism activities. The household earnings yielded through different livelihood options are important indicators of their quality. In this context, tables 5.5 and 5.7 reveal that the average annual income of tourism-involved and non-tourism-involved families registered an increase of 9% and 4% in the Yuksam area and 39% and 2% in the Khecheopalri over a period of just one year (1997 to 1998). A sizable amount of the revenue (55%) in Yuksam area came from employment in trekking and mountaineering as portorage (Rs. 2755856, equivalent to US$67216), followed by grocery shop (Rs. 663749, equivalent to US$1'6189), hotels/lodges/tea stalls (Rs. 1574933, equivalent to US$38413), and very minimum to local guides (Rs. 24887, equivalent to US$607) in 1998. The tourism sector is the most important source of revenue generation, followed by the service sector and agriculture (Tables 5.5 & 5.7). The pattern is similar for both sites. In the agriculture sector, about 50% of the total household income comes from large cardamom alone. However, it may be argued that the household income alone, without taking cognizance of the number of employment days, fails to truly reflect the quality of different livelihood options. Thus, the foregoing discussions reveal that an all-around socio-economic development has taken place in both sites, leading from one sector to another and so on.

The average annual income of all the stakeholders in the Yuksam Dzongri-Goechha La corridor and the Khecheopalri Lake is Rs. 25994 (US$634) and Rs. 14924 (US$364), respectively (average of one year worked out on the basis of constant prices prevalent in the year). The tourism sector in the Yuksam area contributes the maximum with its share of 70%, whereas the service sector accounts for only 18% and the rest of the contribution comes from farm activities. Although the income of pack animal operators and teashop owners decreased due to low domestic visitation numbers in 1998, it continued to dominate the hotel/lodge and porters, whose income increased by 52% and 6%, respectively. Regarding the Khecheopalri Lake area, the maximum revenue (54%) is generated through farm activities, while 30% comes from the tourism sector, and the rest from other sources. It is often said that the economic gains from trekking tourism are more evenly and quickly distributed throughout a regional economy than other types of tourism. This is evidenced by the fact that much of the gain derived from accommodation and portorage stays within the local community.

5.4.2. Quality of Life

It is clearly shown that the quality of life enjoyed by households in the hotels/lodges is far superior to that enjoyed by their counterparts. For example, per capita expenditure on superior grains, fruits and vegetables, clothing and so on is much better in hotel/lodge owning families (Table 5.5 & 5.8). Per capita expenditure on education is also higher among hotel/lodge owners than among other stakeholders. An increase in the level of education over a period of time is also an important and qualitative indicator of economic development. Most of the families who own hotels/lodges have sent their children to Gangtok, Darjeeling, and other cities in India for better education. Even though people involved in tourism are economically much better off, their traditions and culture, such as dress, marriage, food habits, and so on, are still intact. This is in contrast to other transformed areas, e.g., Himachal Pradesh, where economic prosperity has dealt a severe blow to these values (Sharma, 1996).

The food habits of the people at both sites showed some changes during 1997 and 1998. Though the farming system continues to be dominated by maize and potatoes, maize is no longer the staple diet of the people. Practically all households have switched over to rice, though the rice eaten by them is of poor quality. The factors which led to this change are due to an increase in both off-farm and on-farm employment opportunities. While more off-farm jobs have become available in the tourism sector, the on-farm employment opportunities have received a boost with the spread of the large cardamom and vegetable cultivation. This has led to an increase in incomes and changes in expenditure patterns.

5.4.3. Consumption Pattern

The change in economic structure brought about by tourism profoundly altered the consumption patterns of all stakeholders at both sites. The changes in food consumption are another indicator of economic development in the area. The dietary changes in the Yuksam-Dzongri-Goechha La and the Khecheopalri Lake areas during 1997-1998 have received some attention. It is very difficult to measure the changes in the consumption of the diet over time or over space and relate it to economic development. Human beings eat an astonishing variety of foods. One way to make this complexity more easily understood is to group foods into classes, such as cereals or dairy products, and measure their relative importance based on their caloric content. Even so, classifying the stakeholder-wise diets of more than 200 households causes difficulties. There would thus seem to be an obvious relationship between diet and economic development. The dietary pattern of mountain people is different from that of the general population, as consumption of a variety of roots, tubers, green leafy vegetables, and livestock products is higher in their diet. Fruits and vegetables have a very low caloric and protein content per unit weight, and cannot play the role of a staple food. Pulses provide a good source of protein and have a high caloric content. They are found in nearly all traditional diets as a complement.

A change in consumption patterns and their relationship to changes in income structure were not properly analyzed earlier. However, evidence suggests that consumption patterns increase in the early stages of economic growth (FAO, 1958). An increase in incomes leads to different patterns of consumption at different stages of economic growth. In the study area before 1990, the majority of the population was very poor, and most of the limited incomes had to be spent upon rice and potatoes, the cheapest sources of calories. Hence, any increase in incomes led not only to the purchase of more expensive foods to add diversity to a monotonous diet but also to an increase in the consumption of meat. The total food caloric supply in study sites increased from 1878 kcal to 1881 kcal in tourism-involved families and from 1764 to 1827 kcal in non-tourism-involved families in the Yuksam area, and from 1822 to 1987 kcal in tourism-involved families and from 1593 to 1787 kcal in non-tourism-involved families in the Khecheopalri Lake area during 1997 to 1998. This showed a 0.16% increase in tourism-involved families and a 3.51% increase in non-tourism-involved families in the Yuksam area, as well as a 9.05% increase in tourism-involved families and a 12.18% increase in non-tourism-involved families in the Khecheopalri Lake area. Variation in caloric intake by different stakeholders is presented in figure 5.2.

A minor decrease in caloric intake is recorded among pack animal operators and fair price shop stakeholders due to a decrease in the number of domestic visitors and HMI trainees in the Yuksam-Dzongri-Goechha La corridor. According to estimates, meat contributed 127 kcal and 87 kcal (6.76% to 4.93%) to the average daily per capita calorie supply in 1997 in tourism and non-tourism-based households at Yukasam. Cereals such as rice or wheat, on the other hand, contributed 1112 kcal and 1123 kcal (59% and 64%). Milk and milk products provided 163 kcal and 128 kcal per person per day (Table 5.9). All this has changed in tourism and non-tourism-involved families at both sites. The per capita consumption of meat increased from 6.76% to 7.28% among tourism-involved families during 1997-98. The per capita supply of pulses has decreased in tourism-involved families in the Yuksam site, while the supply of milk and milk products has increased. Vegetables and fruits, for instance, now contribute 4% to the average calorie supply. Tourism-based affluence has led to increased economic differentiation in wealth at both the sites and household levels. For one decade, villages have differed sharply not only in the percentage of households with earnings from trekking and mountaineering, but also in the percentage of households with income from services and businesses. With increased affluence, the area's average diet will change further, becoming similar to that of other developed Asian countries in future. Food preferences at both sites are changing rapidly. Today, people not only eat significantly more meat than they did earlier, but there is also a trend towards a more diverse diet.

To examine the trends among different stakeholders, calories derived from various sources are plotted against income per capita per month (Figure 5.3). It is clear from figure 5.3 that economic growth has led to an increased consumption pattern. Increases in income prompt consumers to purchase more of the expensive foods, such as sugar, alcoholic beverages, oils, fruits, vegetables, meats, fish, and dairy products.

Regressing the calorie intake against income yields a positive correlation with as much as 84% to 92% being influenced by income (r2 0.837 and r2 0.919) (Figure 5.4), suggesting a moderately close relationship between calories and income per capita. Results show that economic development leads to changes in food consumption as income grows. With an increase in income, total caloric intake and the consumption of other foods increase.

5.4.4. Household Assets

The asset's inventory of sample households, representing different stakeholders in terms of residential buildings, cattlesheds, electronic goods, and utensils, is another indicator of economic development. The amount of assets per stakeholder is more in the Yuksam area than in the Khecheoplari area because visitors stay in the Yuksam area longer and they spend more money. In the composition and relative importance of different assets in both areas, residential buildings account for more. The most crucial difference, however, is in the percentage of non-farm assets, such as televisions, vehicles, and other durable household goods. Stakeholder-wise significant changes are observed in porters and hotel/lodge-owning families due to an increase in wage rates and more days and times spent trekking.

5.5. Conclusion

The growth of visitors has been responsible for significant changes in employment and income generation, leading to improved socio-economic conditions for the local people and a positive impact on the overall national and state GDP. In economically depressed areas, the employment and income generated by tourism may help mitigate out-migration.

Agriculture is still the main occupation of the villagers at both sites. Crop yield is very low, and people purchase food from the market to meet their daily demand. Now the people of Yuksam and Khecheopalri have reoriented their local economy around tourism. In 1997, about 46% and 7% of the households had income from this source. However, involvement in tourism-related activities rose to 69% and 22% in 1998 at both sites.

Economic development leads to a change in food consumption patterns as income grows. With an increase in income, total caloric intake and the consumption of other foods increase. When a threshold income growth per capita is reached, further increases in income are devoted to purchasing other food items, such as animal products, fruits, vegetables, and sugar.

Age-Group	Yuksam-Dzongri-Goecha La trekking corridor			Khecheopalri Lake		
	Male	Female	Total	Male	Female	Total
0 – 9	9.60	9.47	19.08	13.12	11.32	24.43
10 – 19	9.10	8.78	17.87	10.18	8.82	19.03
20 – 29	8.84	8.10	16.92	8.82	7.01	15.83
30 – 39	8.39	8.14	16.53	8.83	6.33	15.15
40 – 49	6.74	6.80	13.54	7.01	5.88	12.89
50 – 59	4.89	4.53	9.44	3.62	4.53	8.14
Above 60	3.12	3.50	6.62	1.81	2.72	4.53
Total	50.68	49.32	100	53.39	46.61	100

Table 5.1: Age-sex Composition (%) in 1998

Stakeholders	Sites: Yuksam-Dzongri-Goechha La trekking corridor		Sites: Khecheopalri Lake	
	Male	Female	Male	Female
Tourism involved				
Hotel/Lodges	61.29	38.71	75.00	25.00
Pack-animal operator	57.41	42.59	-	-
Poterage	57.15	42.85	-	-
Fair-price Shop	62.50	37.50	66.66	33.34
Tea Stall	66.66	33.34	45.45	54.55
Non-Tourism	56.00	44.00	56.70	43.30
Total	53.41	46.59	56.75	43.25

Table 5.2: Percent Literacy Rate of Stakeholders in 1998

Sites	Paddy	Maize	Wheat	Millet	Barley	Potato/other vegetables	Total	Other foods	Grand Total
Yuksam-Dzongri-Goechha La trekking corridor									
Cropped Area (ha) [1]	15.75	98.135	64.38	28.37	7.25	21.44	235.325	-	-
Average Yield (tonne/ha)	0.50	0.98	0.86	0.37	0.198	0.74	-	-	-
Gross Production (tonne)	7.875	96.172	15.366	10.49	1.43	15.86	187.193	-	-
Less (Crop residuals/other) [2]	0.787	9.617	5.536	1.04	0.143	1.586	18.709	-	-
Net Balance (tonne)	7.088	86.555	49.830	9.450	1.287	14.274	168.484	-	-
Consumable Proportion (%) [3]	85	80	75	90	90	95	-	-	-
Consumable proportion (tonne)	5.902	67.3	35.984	8.320	1.14	13.48	132.136	-	-
Energy Supplied (kJ/g)	14.6	14.4	13.7	13.7	14.0	3.38	-	-	-
Total Energy (J)	86.1692	969.26	492.98	113.98	15.96	45.56	1723.90	-	-
Energy/person/day (MJ) [4]	-	-	-	-	-	-	1.09	0.66	1.75
Khecheopalri Lake									
Cropped Area (ha) [1]	-	47.36	10.85	3.04	1.25	5.51	68.010		
Average Yield (tonne/ha)	-	0.98	0.86	0.37	0.198	0.74	-		
Gross Production (tonne)	-	46.4128	9.331	1.1248	0.2475	4.0774	61.1935		
Less (Crop residuals/other) [2]	-	4.6412	0.9331	0.1124	0.0247	0.4077	6.1191		
Net Balance (tonne)	-	41.4716	8.3979	1.0112	0.228	3.6697	54.7784		
Consumable Proportion (%) [3]	-	95	85	90	85	95	-		
Consumable proportion (tonne)	-	39.450	6.9982	0.8992	0.1852	3.4654	50.998		
Energy Supplied (kJ/g)	-	14.4	13.7	13.7	14	3.38	-		
Total Energy (J)	-	568.08	95.875	12.3190	2.5928	11.7130	690.5798		
Energy/person/day (MJ) [4]	-						1.56	0.66	2.22

1= Primary Survey, 2 = Rents, Storage and residual losses together calculated as 10 %, 3= Consumable proportion is calculated by asking the local community the amount of consumption from the total production, 4= Other foods include mainly sugar, meat, fruit, vegetable oil, milk and milk products etc., and are calculated as c. 15 (%) (Mahat, et al.1987)

Table 5.3: Daily Average Per Capita Food Intake in 1998

Stakeholder	Yuksam-Dzongri-Goechha La trekking corridor		Khecheopalri Lake	
	Number	(%)	Number	(%)
Tourism involved				
Poterage	289	18.56	2	0.79
Pack-animal operator	302	19.40	-	-
Hotel/Lodge	38	2.44	-	-
Fair-price Shop	55	3.53	8	3.16
Tea Stall	7	0.45	-	-
Non-tourism	866	55.62	243	96.05
Total	1557	100	253	100

Table 5.4: Stakeholder Wise Ownership of Livestock in 1998

Parameters	Stakeholders											
	S1		S2		S3		S4		S5		NS	
	1997	1998	1997	1998	1997	1998	1997	1998	1997	1998	1997	1998
Tourism												
Mean	57375	87350	30555	27264	7035	7487	8281	7503	5717	5472	-	-
Median	30500	29750	29000	2667	6995	8097	7250	5833	4500	4500	-	-
Std.Dev.	83922	174518	8504	7148	2448	2502	3702	4703	4559	4436	-	-
Sum	459000	698800	825000	736120	773825	823626	132500	120050	62890	60195	-	-
% of Variation	52.24		-10.77		6.43		-9.39		-4.28		-	
Agriculture												
Mean	8400	9626	7850	8729	5777	5974	7937	8206	-	-	9544	9950
Median	8000	9980	8500	8571	5800	6457	7000	6925	-	-	7500	8754
Std.Dev.	8253	8478	5299	4144	3006	1993	4131	4478	-	-	5667	5666
Sum	58800	67380	211950	235678	618140	657189	63500	65650	-	-	906690	945295
% of Variation	14.59		11.19		6.31		3.38		-		4.25	
Service												
Mean	109000	115750	7000	8783	-	-	30000	21253	-	-	24665	25196
Median	67500	77250	9000	10500	-	-	39000	21854	-	-	24000	24000
Std.Dev.	113140	113077	6245	8063	-	-	20199	8661	-	-	14260	14499
Sum	436000	463000	21000	26350	-	-	120000	138000	-	-	641300	655100
% of Variation	6.19		25.47		-		15.00		-		2.15	
Others												
Mean	22187	25044	4644	4111	1799	1760	19512	21253	7483	7745	7018	7595
Median	17500	17500	3700	3600	1670	1905	19750	21854	6400	6500	4800	4902
Std.Dev.	20329	111240	4779	2463	955	605	8298	8661	3038	3407	9223	11706
Sum	177500	200350	116100	110990	165530	193650	312200	340043	82310	85197	501770	564986
% of Variation	12.87		-4.40		17		8.91		3.50		1259	
Total												
Mean	141412	178691	41056	41086	14164	14969	39387	41484	13200	13217	20498	21296
Median	104250	112240	42000	40360	15575	16193	32500	32775	10000	10392	14825	15650
Std.Dev.	124779	190438	12158	10920	4886	4998	23943	27370	7196	7422	15991	17694
Sum	1131300	1429530	1108514	1109328	1558009	1646553	630200	663743	145200	145392	2049760	2129600
% of Variation	26.36		0.07		5.68		-4.19		0.13		3.89	

S1=Hotel/Lodges; S2=Pack-animal Operator; S3=Porters; S4=Fair Price Shop; S5=Tea Stall; NS=Non-tourism

Table 5.5: Income (Rs) from Various Sources and Percent Variation during 1997 and 1998 among Stakeholders in the Yuksam-Dzongri-Goechha La Trekking Corridor

Parameters	Stakeholders											
	S1		S2		S3		S4		S5		NS	
	1997	1998	1997	1998	1997	1998	1997	1998	1997	1998	1997	1998
Tourism related												
Mean	15354	15606	7250	6993	405	428	12559	14012	5700	5836	-	-
Median	10000	8925	7809	7000	445	463	12500	13575	4000	4000	-	-
Std.Dev.	19225	22107	2332	1981	140	143	5693	6795	3635	3925	-	-
Sum	122833	124850	210855	187509	44514	47044	200950	224191	62700	64200	-	-
% of Variation	1.64		-11.07		5.68		11.56		2.39		-	
Farming												
Mean	2800	3208	2053	2281	683	1025	2712	3040	-	-	3795	4252
Median	2667	3327	1889	2131	660	1029	3100	3500	-	-	2945	3130
Std.Dev.	2751	2826	1458	1157	237	204	1130	1246	-	-	2359	3515
Sum	19600	22460	55418	57432	56730	85092	21700	24320	-	-	379512	425160
% of Variation	14.59		3.63		49.99		12.07		-		12.02	
Food												
Mean	18850	19322	14747	13765	6641	6804	10299	10807	4004	3658	9715	10629
Median	15000	15925	14567	13402	7102	7360	10758	11452	3000	3000	7412	7825
Std.Dev.	7549	7695	3748	3392	2114	2272	3535	3526	1691	1943	6451	8799
Sum	150800	154580	398183	361859	730531	748433	164783	172915	44050	40240	971530	1062900
% of Variation	2.50		-9.12		2.45		4.93		-8.64		9.40	
Non-food												
Mean	3900	4384	4740	4419	1894	1871	3595	3906	832	862	2960	3189
Median	3750	4440	4330	4500	2000	2024	3711	4097	550	535	2224	2347
Std.Dev.	1442	1702	1127	1118	736	625	1256	1330	514	560	2034	2637
Sum	31200	35070	127986	119329	208322	205819	57521	62495	9150	9483	296009	318870
% of Variation	12.40		-6.76		-1.20		8.64		3.63		7.72	
Misleaneous												
Mean	3625	4235	2149	2034	567	599	1947	2146	591	591	1742	638
Median	3500	3550	2150	2065	623	648	1975	2125	600	600	1186	470
Std.Dev.	2048	2637	539	525	195	200	606	629	102	102	1634	527
Sum	29000	33880	58019	54928	62370	65862	31150	34332	6500	6500	174205	63774
% of Variation	16.82		-5.32		5.59		10.21		-		-63.39	
Total												
Mean	44179	46335	31498	29896	10022	10475	29756	32391	11127	10947	18212	18707
Median	41750	44353	31567	28931	10688	11467	30519	33246	8100	8135	13787	13772
Std.Dev.	25164	28700	8050	7429	3449	3680	10472	11555	5516	5979	12235	15469
Sum	353433	370840	850461	781151	1102468	1152251	476105	518253	122400	120423	1821256	1870704
% of Variation	4.92		-8.14		4.51		8.85		-1.61		2.71	

S1=Hotel/Lodges; S2=Pack-animal Operator; S3=Porters; S4=Fair Price Shop; S5=Tea Stall; NS=Non-tourism

Table 5.6: Expenditure (Rs) in Various Items and Percent Variation during 1997 and 1998 among Stakeholders in the Yuksam-Dzongri-Goecha La Trekking Corridor

Parameters	Stakeholders											
	S1		S2		S3		S4		S5		NS	
	1997	1998	1997	1998	1997	1998	1997	1998	1997	1998	1997	1998
Tourism												
Mean	-	-	-	-	-	-	17000	20325	7496	10080	-	-
Median	-	-	-	-	-	-	17000	20325	5000	5550	-	-
Std.Dev.	-	-	-	-	-	-	2121	6116	6218	10046	-	-
Sum	55000	86650	-	-	-	-	34000	40650	37480	50400	-	-
% of Variation	57.54		-		-		19.55		34.47		-	
Agriculture												
Mean	-	-	-	-	-	-	9775	10150	3050	3050	9205	9319
Median	-	-	-	-	-	-	9775	10150	3050	3050	8800	8850
Std.Dev.	-	-	-	-	-	-	2510	2121	71	71	4340	4083
Sum	6500	7650	-	-	-	-	19550	20300	6100	6100	543085	549825
% of Variation	17.69		-		-		3.83				1.24	
Service												
Mean	-	-	-	-	-	-	-	-	-	-	9183	11000
Median	-	-	-	-	-	-	-	-	-	-	12000	15000
Std.Dev.	-	-	-	-	-	-	-	-	-	-	8149	9644
Sum	36000	50400	-	-	-	-	36000	42000	-	-	27500	33000
% of Variation	40		-		-		16.66		-		20	
Others												
Mean	-		-	-	-	-	925	2700	1925	2190	4864	4816
Median	- -		-	-	-	-	925	2705	1750	2105	3725	4150
Std.Dev.	-		-	-	-	-	813	3330	789	606	3487	2934
Sum	1500	4300	-	-	-	-	1850	5410	7700	8760	163885	166185
% of Variation	138.88		-		-		192.43		13.76		1.40	
Total												
Mean	-	-	-	-	-	-	47300	55930	10256	13052	11477	11703
Median	-	-	-	-	-	-	47300	55930	7500	10926	10500	10750
Std.Dev.	-	-	-	-	-	-	23613	29599	7084	8550	5587	5011
Sum	89400	149000	-	-	-	-	94600	111860	51280	65260	734520	749010
% of Variation	50.50		-		-		18.24		27.26		1.97	

S1=Hotel/Lodges; S2=Pack-animal Operator; S3=Porters; S4=Fair Price Shop; S5=Tea Stall; NS=Non-tourism

Table 5.7: Income (Rs) from Various Sources and Percent Variation during 1997 and 1998 among Stakeholders in the Khecheopalri Lake

Parameters	S1 1997	S1 1998	S2 1997	S2 1998	S3 1997	S3 1998	S4 1997	S4 1998	S5 1997	S5 1998	NS 1997	NS 1998
Tourism related												
Mean	-	-	-	-	-	-	9175	11000	2630	4156	-	-
Median	-	-	-	-	-	-	9175	11000	1500	2650	-	-
Std.Dev.	-	-	-	-	-	-	3783	5657	2741	4859	-	-
Sum	25000	38580	-	-	-	-	18350	22000	13150	20780	-	-
% of Variation	54.32		-		-		19.89		58.02		-	
Farming												
Mean	-	-		-	-	-	4325	5000	825	875	2850	2904
Median	-	-		-	-	-	4325	5000	825	875	2625	2687
Std.Dev.	-	-		-	-	-	1662	2121	35	106	1287	1196
Sum	2000	2250		-	-	-	8650	10000	1650	1750	182380	185891
% of Variation	12.50		-		-		1560		6.66		1.92	
Food												
Mean	-	-		-	-	-	15775	17030	4830	5140	5643	5757
Median	-	-		-	-	-	15775	17030	3750	4500	5250	5375
Std.Dev.	-	-		-	-	-	7036	6321	2885	3089	2299	2275
Sum	22000	25650		-	-	-	31550	34060	24150	25700	361160	368441
% of Variation	16.59		-		-		7.95		6.41		2.01	
Non-food												
Mean	-	-		-	-	-	5720	6250	1027	1255	1710	1743
Median	-	-		-	-	-	5720	6250	1050	1215	1575	1612
Std.Dev.	-	-		-	-	-	5487	5303	352	473	772	717
Sum	7500	8750		-	-	-	11440	12500	5135	6274	109428	111535
% of Variation	16.66		-		-		9.26		22.18		1.92	
Misiennenus												
Mean	-	-		-	-	-	3311	3375	718	730	798	813
Median	-	-		-	-	-	3311	3375	525	567	735	752
Std.Dev.	-	-		-	-	-	1653	1590	496	439	360	335
Sum	6500	6500		-	-	-	6622	6750	3590	3651	51066	52050
% of Variation			-		-		1.93		1.69		1.92	
Total												
Mean	-	-		-	-	-	38306	42655	9535	11411	11000	11217
Median	-	-		-	-	-	38306	42655	6700	7400	10185	10427
Std.Dev.	-	-	-	-	-	-	16297	16751	6620	8835	4707	4515
Sum	63000	81730		-	-	-	76612	85310	47674	57055	704034	717916
% of Variation	29.73		-		-		11.35		19.67		1.97	

S1=Hotel/Lodges; S2=Pack-animal Operator; S3=Porters; S4=Fair Price Shop; S5=Tea Stall; NS=Non-tourism

Table 5.8: Expenditure (Rs) in Various Items and Percent Variation during 1997 and 1998 among Stakeholders in the Khecheopalri Lake

Food-items	Yuksam-Dzongri-Goechha La Corridor				Khecheopalri Lake			
	Kcal per person per day							
	Tourism		Non-Tourism		Tourism		Non-Tourism	
	1997	1998	1997	1998	1997	1998	1997	1998
Cereals	1112.16	1126.00	1123.20	1153.20	1108.20	1128.00	1118.40	1140.00
Pulses	64.28	57.72	63.32	65.60	63.41	78.72	32.80	32.80
Leafy Vegetables	41.40	43.40	47.00	50.00	40.00	46.66	42.00	48.00
Other Vegetables	34.20	33.80	28.00	25.00	29.66	34.33	15.00	20.00
Root and Tubers	26.22	33.06	28.50	33.25	32.61	41.48	98.40	158.76
Milk Products	162.73	158.47	127.80	127.80	224.83	253.23	71.00	92.30
Fat & Oils	210.60	210.90	180.00	198.00	147.00	195.00	90.00	135.00
Sugar & Jaggery	85.42	80.13	79.38	86.94	74.34	83.16	37.80	49.14
Meat	126.96	137.44	87.30	87.30	101.95	126.23	87.39	110.69
Grand Total	1877.97	1880.92	1764.50	1827.09	1822.00	1986.81	1592.79	1786.69

Table 5.9: Average Daily Food Calorie Supply at the Study Sites During 1997 and 1998

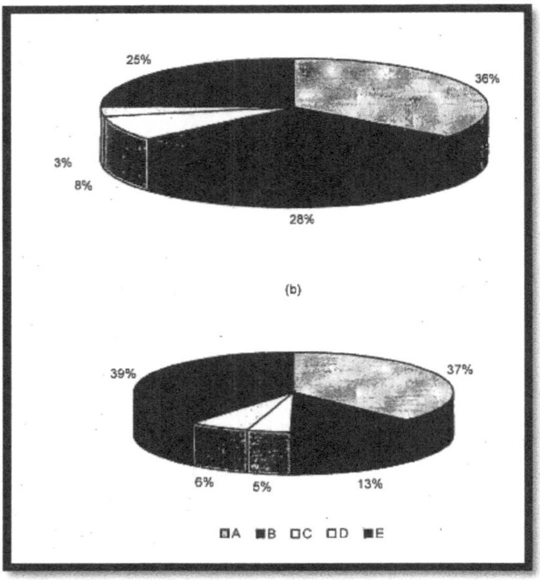

Figure 5.1: Land Utilization Pattern of Study Area (a) Yuksam and (b) Khecheopalri Villages, 1997 (A: Net Area Shown, B: Fallow Land, C: Other Cultivated Land Excluding Fallow Land, D: Area Not Available for Cultivation, E: Forest)

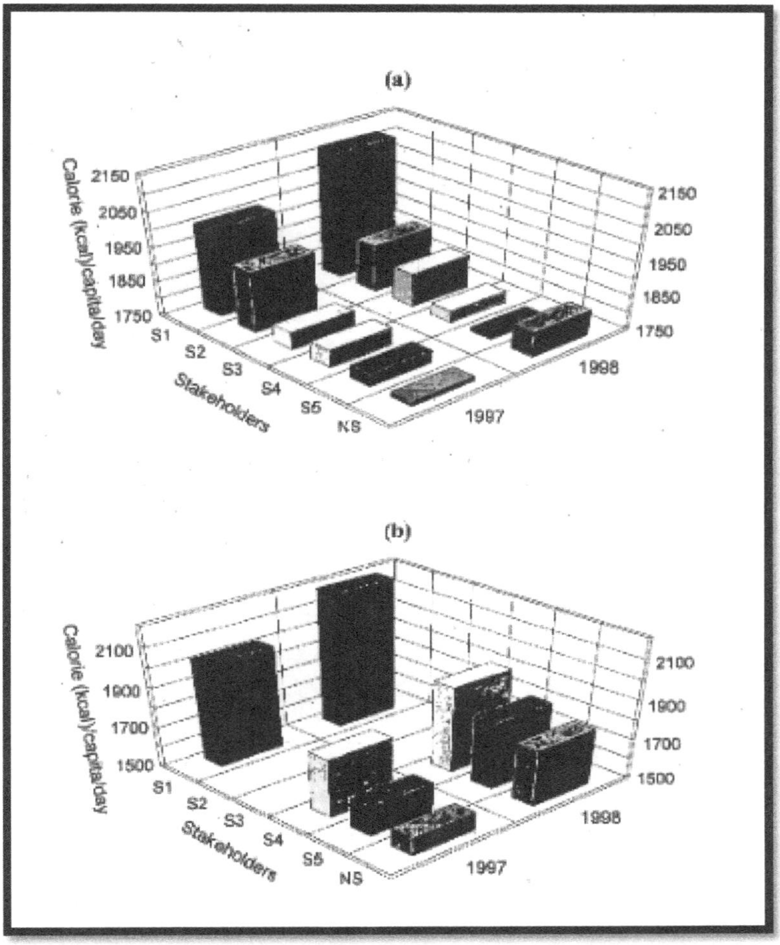

Figure 5.2: Variation in Calorie Intake by Different Stakeholders in (a) Yuksam-Dzongri-Gochha La Trekking Corridor and (b) The Khecheopalri Lake

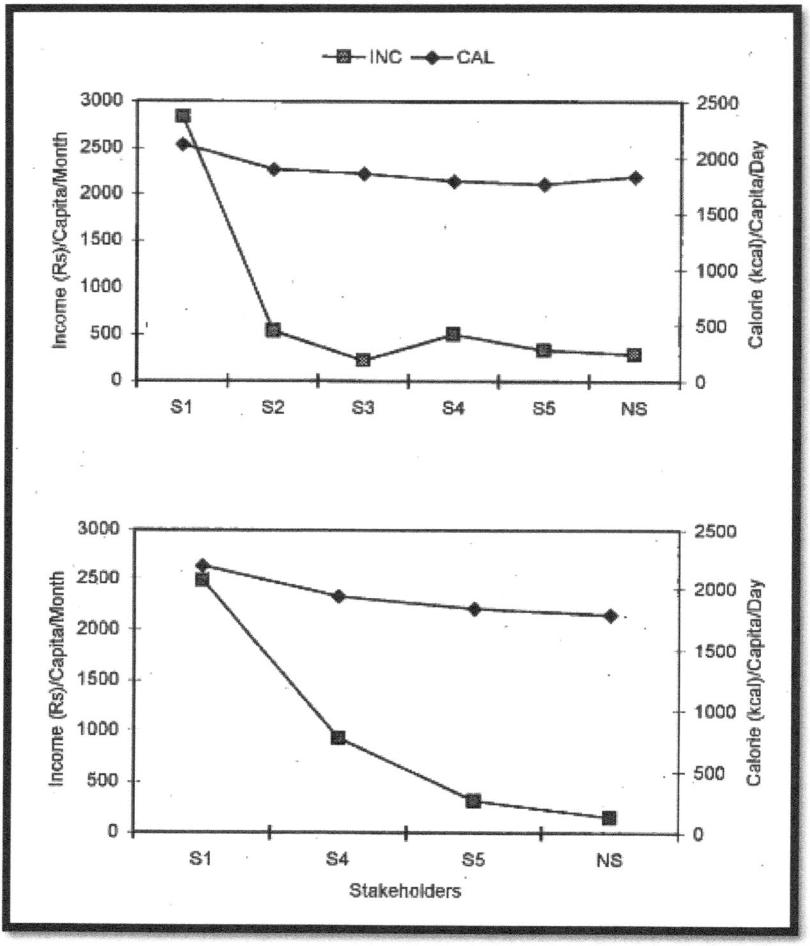

Figure 5.3: Calories (kcal)/Capita/Day and Income (Rs) Level per Capita/Month in (a) Yuksam-Dzongri-Gochha La Trekking Corridor and (b) The Khecheopalri Lake by Stakeholders

S1=Hotel/Lodges; S2=Pack-animal Operators; S3=Porters; S4=Fair price shop; S5=Tea

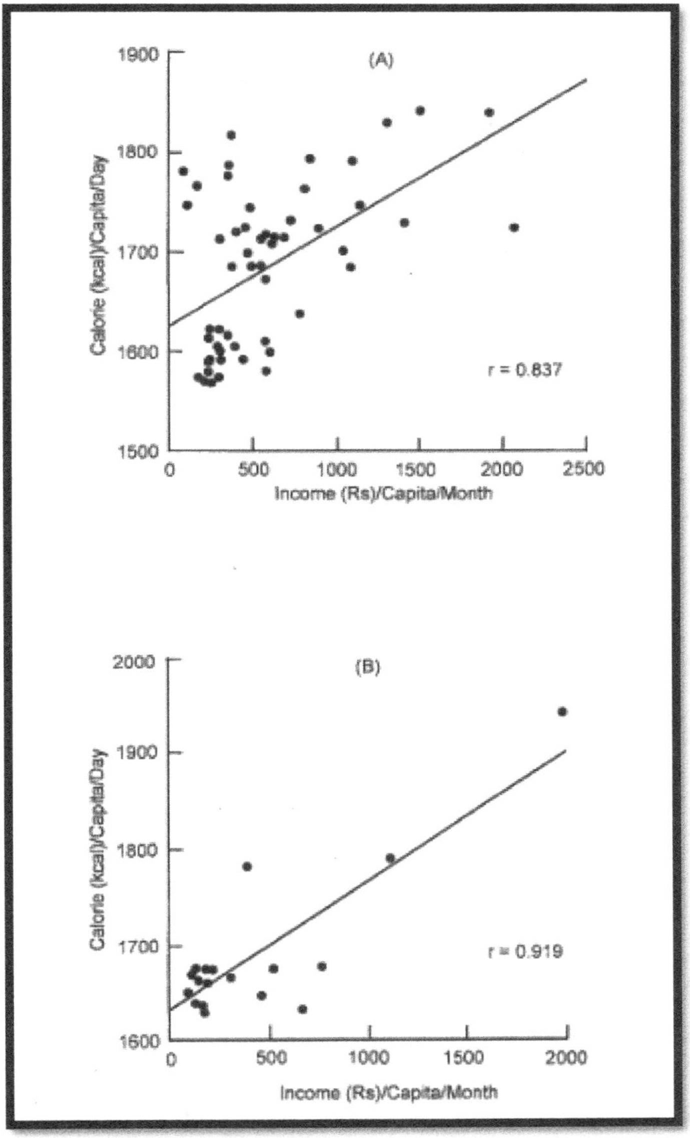

Figure 5.4: Relationship between Income Per Capita and Absolute Consumption in (A) Yuksam-Dzongri-Gochha La Trekking Corridor and (B) The Khecheopalri Lake

Chapter 6 | Evaluation of Environmental Damage to Natural Ecosystems

6.1. Introduction

The rapidly growing population and increasing number of visitors have put tremendous pressure on the forests. Over the past three decades, a growing debate has emerged regarding the impact of tourism on developing countries. Mountaineering and trekking have recently had adverse impacts on the environment of high-altitude areas (Jeffries, 1982; Pawson et al., 1984; Karan & Mather, 1985; Banskota & Upadhyay, 1991; Zurick, 1992; and Rai & Sundriyal, 1997). The overuse of forest resources has led to environmental threats in the Hindu-Kush Himalayan region (Thapa & Weber, 1990; Willis & Garrod, 1991; Singh & Singh, 1992). Dependence on fuelwood for energy is causing a serious deforestation problem in national parks, wilderness, and other protected areas. Natural areas represent efforts to preserve our natural heritage from further exploitation and degradation. Such areas also provide greater recreational opportunities. Protected areas of biodiversity interest provide a variety of benefits and services, which are essential for the economic development of a region.

Monetary valuation of any natural ecosystem is very difficult (Bergström et al., 1990; Dixon et al., 1994). In past, these areas were valued only for products such as timber, fuel, fodder and non-timber forest produce. The intangible benefits of these areas have not been properly accounted for by policymakers while implementing development programs in developing countries. However, in developed countries, economic valuations of natural resources have been used in the conservation and management of protected areas (Pearce et al., 1994; Wilson & Carpenter, 1999). Contingent valuation methods were widely applied in estimating the economic value of both marketed and non-marketed goods (Brookshire et al., 1983; Majid et al., 1983; Walsh et al., 1986; Dixon & Sherman, 1990).

The present chapter particularly deals with the quantitative assessment of current forest and other land-use, fuel, fodder, and timber consumption patterns, the impact of resource extraction on the health of the trail and lake, the economic valuation of the biologically rich forests of the trekking corridor and the Lake site, valuing the recreational/sacredness benefits of the lake, and applying the economic model of travel cost and contingent valuation methods. The estimation can prove useful for the added costs of fuelwood, fodder, and timber management prescriptions needed to protect the critical habitats of the Sikkim Himalaya. An attempt has also been made to demonstrate the practicality of developing WTP functions for managers in estimating the benefits of other environmental values of forests, such as soil erosion and recreation.

6.2. Methods

6.2.1. Analysis of Forest and Other Land-Use/Covers

Satellite imagery (1: 50000), IRS-IA/IB, LISS-II and IRS-IC, FCC of bands 2, 3 and 4 were interpreted for forest cover and other land-use/cover maps of the Yuksam-Dzongri-Goechha La Corridor and Sacred Khecheopalri Lake employing a photo interpretation technique for the years 1988 and 1997, in conjunction with the Survey of India topographical maps (1: 50000). Intensive field investigations were carried out to check the land-use/cover for ground truth verification. Areas of different forest types and other land-use categories were quantified using a digital planimeter.

6.2.2 Extraction of Forest Products

The study is based on a detailed primary survey conducted in 1997 and 1998. The fuelwood used and the extraction of species by different stakeholders were based on a detailed survey. The samples were selected from different stakeholders using a stratified random sampling method. A total of 129 stakeholders, consisting of 39 households from the local communities, followed by 5 hotels/lodges, 2 groups (127 trainees and 37 staff members) of HMI trainees, 8 travel agents, 45 FITs, 6 pack animal operators and 24 porters, participated from the Yuksam-Dzongri-Goechha La trekking corridor. On the other hand, a total of 15 stakeholders, comprising 10 households from the local community, 1 trekker hut, and 4 tea/grocery shops, participated from the sacred Khecheopalri Lake. To provide proportionate representation to every socio-economic segment, the community households were stratified based on the size of landholding, income status, ethnicity, and caste, reflecting social status. Stakeholder-wise fuelwood consumption per day in each season (summer, monsoon and winter), supply of fuelwood from different sources, time taken and distance covered in fuelwood collection were collected through a questionnaire survey.

The questionnaire is the most widely adopted method for gathering data on the collection and consumption quantities of fuelwood. The widespread use of questionnaires is likely due to limitations in time, resources, and logistical facilities (Uma Shanker et al., 1998). Although extensively used, the questionnaire method generates highly biased data because most respondents do not provide accurate information due to a lack of interest, inadequate knowledge of the subject, and intentional distortion of information. Inadequate knowledge of quantities might also lead to incorrect reporting (Malhotra et al., 1991). However, the questionnaire method is useful for rapid assessment and collecting qualitative information, such as the names of species used for fuelwood. To avoid biases, the estimation of the actual quantity of fuelwood requirement/consumption by each stakeholder was worked out on the basis of personal observation over a period of 24 hours by adopting a weight survey method. Simultaneously, observations were also made in each sample to quantify fuelwood use for various tasks such as cooking, water heating and other purposes. During the survey, the interviewer visited each sample stakeholder and requested the head of the family to monitor the amount of fuelwood that would be burnt during that particular day. The wood was weighed by a spring balance and then left in the kitchen (30 kg wood bundle) of each stakeholder with instructions to burn wood only from the given bundle. The next day, the interviewer returned to each sample household, weighed the remaining wood, and deducted it from the original bundle to calculate the actual daily consumption. The time spent collecting fog fuelwood was noted when the household members went to the forest. People's responses to the resource pressure they faced, considered to be the most accurate indicators of fuel shortages, were used to examine the severity of the fuelwood problem.

The quantification of biomass utilization was focused on the stall fed fodder consumption. The magnitude of this is important because it is closely related, linked and represents the primary direct removal of biomass from the forest. Fodder demand was estimated throughout the year. This was achieved through a survey of headloads (weight and composition) collected on a daily basis by each household at both sites.

Participatory Rural Appraisal (PRA) techniques were also used to collect information on preferred species for fuel, fodder, and timber through group and key informant discussions. The estimates of the average amount of each forest product collected give some indication of the total volume of non-timber forest product (NTFP). The people's response to the resource pressure they faced, considered to be one of the most accurate indicators of resource shortage, was used to examine the severity of the problem.

6.2.3. Trail and Lake Site Erosion

Trail erosion refers specifically to assessments of processes and consequences of soil erosion on the trail tread and lake. Soil loss is particularly important because it is not self-limiting, unlike many other forms of trail impact. The entire trail and the Lake site have been visited to select the observation sites. First, an assessment was made of the trail surface conditions at a sampling point, including trail width, as well as evaluating changes in forest cover and composition. Stratified point sampling is the most common method for trail erosion surveys due to its simplicity of implementation, as noted by Hall & Kuss (1989). The trail side erosion along Yuksam-Dzongri Goechha La corridor was measured from 5 experimental plots along altitudinal gradients, considering slope, aspects, forest density and 12 experimental plots under different land-use/cover combinations in the lake watershed during 1997 and 1998, over three monsoon seasons (pre-monsoon, mid-monsoon and post-monsoon). These were estimated using natural shallow surface runoff channels and artificially delineated plots (Singh et al., 1983; Rai & Sharma, 1998). The delineated plot size was 10*3m for the estimation of overland flow and soil loss. These plots were bounded with aluminum sheets (6 cm. inserted in the soil and remaining 15 cm. exposed in air) on all sides to prevent water from entering from adjacent areas. The plots were located on slopes ranging from 150 to 450. The overland flow and soil losses along the slope were estimated from the collecting tank after each rainfall event. The eroded soils were sampled in the form of sediment settled at the bottom of the collecting tank and as suspended clay material.

6.2.4. Economic Valuation

Several methods are available to evaluate the recreational/sacredness value of natural ecosystems. In this study, two independent methods for valuation of environmental goods, such as the Travel Cost Method (TCM) and the Contingent Valuation Method (CVM), were used. Both methods have been recommended as providing acceptable economic measures of the social benefits of recreational activities for both use and non-use values (Walsh, 1986; Navrud, 1992; Cordell & Bergstrom, 1993). The other method used in this type of assessment is cost-benefit analysis (Ableson, 1979; Kneese, 1984; Haneley & Spash, 1993), but it has a long, controversial history (Hufschmidt et al., 1983). Several models from each of the methods were constructed.

6.2.4.1. Sampling Design and Data Source

The study was based on a random survey of 545 respondents, consisting of 125 domestic visitors, 325 foreign visitors and 95 local community members from Yuksam-Dzongri-Goechha La trekking corridor, and 360 respondents from the Khecheopalri Lake site, consisting of 50 members of the local community, 140 pilgrims (from within Sikkim), 95 domestic and 75 foreign visitors in 1997-98. The categories of respondents were international tourists, termed as foreign; Indian tourists, termed as domestic; and the people living in the area, termed as the local community. Out of the total, only 243 respondents (31 local people, 50 domestic visitors and 62 foreign visitors) in the trekking corridor and 180 respondents (20 community members, followed by 34 domestic visitors, 51 foreign visitors and 75 pilgrims) showed their willingness-to-pay (WTP) for the conservation and protection of the trekking corridor and lake, while others refused. Travel costs incurred by individuals in visiting the lake were estimated using a sample of 140 pilgrims, who completed travel expense information. The interviews were conducted through a structured questionnaire (Bishop & Heborlein, 1992; Arrow et al., 1993) over a period of six months (March to May and October to December), corresponding with two peak tourist seasons. The sampling was random and took place at various times of the day and on all days of the week to ensure a representative sample. At the outset, the interviewer introduced themselves to the respondents. The respondents were informed about the nature of the work and were assured that their responses would be used for research purposes and that confidentiality would be maintained. A brochure containing general information about the KNP and the Kachoecho Lake area, and about some of the environmentally sensitive issues faced by both sites, was presented at a specific point in the course of the interview. Hence, all the respondents were brought to a minimum level of information about the benefits of preserving and maintaining the sites. This would perhaps act to counter social and peer desirability bias. Face-to-face interviews (Arrow et al., 1993) were conducted at both sites and lasted 30 minutes on average. Adult visitors, who had a defined source of income, were only interviewed because they were considered more realistic in making personal valuations of their recreational/sacredness experiences at the trekking corridor and the Lake site, vis-à-vis their budget constraints (Brown & Henry, 1989). The visitor statistics provided information on socio-economic variables, including age, sex, educational level, occupation, and income.

6.2.4.2. Travel Cost Method

The Travel Cost Method (TCM) has been widely used in valuing freshwater ecosystems (Caulkins et al., 1986; Dixon et al., 1994). It is an indirect valuation method that uses visitors' travel costs to a recreational area as a proxy for the price of the recreational activity, along with participation rates and visitor attributes, to estimate the recreational value of the site. Variations in travel costs and visitation rate can then be used to estimate a demand curve, which is used to compute the consumer surplus of the activity, i.e., the recreational value. The demand curve establishes a function between the price of a good (travel cost) and the quantity of the good consumed (number of visits). It is usually downward sloping because at higher prices, fewer people will visit, while at lower prices, the number of visitors is greater. The consumer surplus or area under the demand curve but above the price, is a measure of the sacred value of the Khecheopalri Lake. Pilgrims and domestic and foreign visitors were distinguished in order to distinguish the pilgrims, who were on a single destination trip to the lake. Outside visitors to Sikkim usually undertake multiple destination trips, which include the Khecheopalri Lake. Therefore, this part of the analysis focused only on the recreational/sacredness value of local pilgrims. This model provides an estimate of the benefits individuals receive from visiting a site by observing their travel-related expenses (Clawson & Knetsch, 1966; Krutilla & Fisher, 1975; Dixon & Sherman, 1991; Freeman, 1993).

Based on the theoretical models, questionnaires were prepared and administered to visitors to the lake. The respondents were asked about the cost of the current trip to the Lake site, the process for deciding about trip destinations, and a series of socio-demographic and economic questions. Additionally, a trip diary was developed, which elicited detailed information on the itinerary, cost, time, and quality of the current trip to the lake. The travel cost to the lake, distance, household income and other socio-economic variables (age, sex, education and density) were included as independent variables in regression models, which were developed at the zone level based on individual visitors' responses. The travel cost method measures the demand function for a visit to a site. A demand function is an empirical relationship between the price of a good and the quantity purchased:

Vi = f (Pi, X)

Where:

Vi = visitation rate of the ith population from each zone that is estimated by dividing the number of visits from the respective zone by the zone population;

Pi = cost of visiting the site from the zone;

X = set of socio-economic variables which might shift the demand function, such as income or age.

On the basis of the above demand function (Equation 1), we developed two equations to estimate the demand curve considering travel cost (T) and distance (D), as other variables such as age, literacy, income and density were not significant factors in visitation rate. The distance between the place of origin and destination was derived from the state motor vehicle department of the Government of Sikkim. The distance was converted into currency by applying the fare rates. The average value in currency for a one-kilometre distance was estimated to calculate the travel cost:

(2)

(3) The linear specification of the above function is:

V= oco + OCIT+ oc2 D+e (4)

Where oc parameters, e = error term which is independent and normally distributed.

Regression analysis was used to estimate the parameters for deriving the equation. The consumer surplus value is the willingness-to-pay over and above the price of the trip by the consumer. This is illustrated in figure 6.1. Tm Vm is the travel cost demand curve. Tm is the maximum travel cost where the visitation rate drops to zero. Vm is the maximum visitation rate at which the travel cost is equal to zero. If Ti is the travel cost for the visitors from the ith population zone, Vi will be the corresponding visitation rate.

The net benefit is the consumer surplus, which represents the additional utility gained over and above the consumer's expenditure (cost) on travel to reach the site. This is the area below the demand curve and above the price of the trip. In the figure, CS(i) (the shaded portion) represents the consumer surplus for visitors from the ith population zone.

Mathematically, the consumer surplus value [CS (i)] can be estimated as:

Tm

CS (i) - f Vi dT (5)

Where:

Vi = visitation rate from the ith population zone,

Ti = actual travel cost from the ith population zone, and

Tm = maximum travel cost the visitors are willing to pay.

The recreational value of the entire site was achieved by summing up the consumer surplus estimates from all observed users. The total annual consumer surplus (ACS) of the recreation site across all the zones was:

ACS = E CS (6) i -1

Where N = the number of surrounding population zones selected for the study.

The annual consumer surplus (ACS) for the pilgrims was estimated using the real rate of interest for the corresponding period; the rate was calculated as the difference between the lending rate of interest of the Reserve Bank of India and the rate of inflation for the year 1997-98.

Therefore, the present value of the ACS can be calculated by:

PV = ACS/r (7)

If the effect of inflation is considered, the real rate of interest (r*) has to be taken instead of the social rate of discount (r).

Therefore,

PV = ACS/r* (8)

6.2.4.3. The Contingent Valuation Method

The contingent valuation method (CVM) attempts to value non-market goods by asking people directly for their willingness-to-pay to obtain specified improvements or to avoid decrements in them, using social scientific survey techniques (Heberlein, 1988; Bishop & Heberlein, 1992; Arrow et al., 1993). The CVM uses a questionnaire or survey to create a hypothetical market or referendum, and then allows the respondents to use it to state or reveal their WTP for recreation, option, existence and bequest values (Mitchell & Carson, 1989; Mullarkey & Bishop, 1995). The CVM survey tended to address a greater diversity of issues related to lake and terrestrial ecosystems. The main concern in using the WTP technique was with the validity of responses; specifically, would the respondents actually pay the money they agreed to pay in the survey?

The contingent valuation method (CVM) remains a subject of heated debate within the non-market valuation literature due to its hypothetical nature (Hanemann, 1994) and susceptibility to biases (Cummings et al., 1986; Mitchell & Carson, 1989; Freeman, 1993). Attempts have been made to minimize the biases in order to get a reliable estimate of the economic value of recreation. One of the most significant potential biases of CVM is scenario misspecification, particularly in valuing the amenity. This is a serious bias in estimating non-use values. In the present study, the bias should have been minimal for use values. Responses were taken only when visitors were familiar with the non-use goods after visiting the trekking corridor and the lake. In-person interviews were initiated by informing respondents about the work and background of the Sikkim Biodiversity and Ecotourism project. Respondents were told about the nature of the project. The nature of the interview was explained, and the issues related to the trekking corridor and the Khecheopalri Lake were introduced. The respondents were also assured that their responses would be used for research purposes and that their confidentiality would be maintained.

The latter would perhaps act to counter social and peer desirability bias. Face-to-face interviews secure a higher response rate than other survey techniques. People did their best to provide honest answers to the CV questions. In the CV exercise, we adopted a double-bounded dichotomous choice (DBDC) formulation, as it is more information-intensive (Hanemann et al., 1991). First, the respondents were asked whether they were willing to pay for the non-market commodity benefits after being given proper information about the commodity. If the answer was 'no', the process ended there with that particular respondent. If the answer was 'yes', then the second step was to determine the maximum amount they were willing to pay. The maximum willingness to pay was determined by the bidding process. The interviewer started the bidding at a particular amount. If it was above their willingness-to-pay, the interviewer reduced the bid gradually until the answer was 'yes' and the value was recorded. If the respondent agreed to the interviewer's initial bidding amount, the interviewer gradually raised the bid until the respondent said 'no'. Respondents who showed an inability to pay in cash were considered for their willingness to actually do service in the trekking corridor and lake. These respondents were asked if they were willing to contribute their time towards the maintenance of the sites. This provided an opportunity for those who could not pay but were willing to do service. Respondents were also asked how many days per year they would be willing to work voluntarily at both the sites.

Socio-economic details were also collected for regression purposes. Apart from name and addresses, information on age, education, occupation and annual income from all sources was also collected. An attempt was also made to establish the importance of environmental issues as perceived by the respondents and to measure whether they demonstrated implicit values for the environment and non-use values. The questionnaire contained questions about the environmental attitudes of the respondents, e.g., how they will rank the justification of biodiversity loss, why they avoided or chose to visit the YuksamDzongri-Goechha La trekking corridor and the Khecheopalri Lake site. These preferences were measured on a five-point scale: "strongly agree", "agree", "neutral", "disagree" and "strongly disagree".

Community-based household information was collected by a primary survey using stratified random sampling. Statistical analysis was done using Systat Version 6.0 (1996), considering all the responses, including those who protested the bid.

6.3. Forest Cover and Density

The five classes of land-use were identified occurring in both sites (Table 6.1). A total of 84% and 77% of the lake and trekking corridor area had forests. The forest cover is divided into conifer, rhododendron, mixed-broad leaf, and alpine scrub and forest blanks. These forests are most predominant in the trail corridor (Table 6.1 & Plates 2c & 2d). The majority (34%) of the forestland is under degraded category (crown cover, 20%), 19% are open forest (crown cover, 21-40%) and 19% are dense forest (crown cover, > 40%), whereas in the Khecheopalri Lake site, it is dominated by open mixed forest (41%), followed by dense mixed (23%) and degraded forest (21%) (Table 6.1).

Agriculture is the predominant non-forest land-use, occupying about 14% of the total area in the trekking corridor and 13% in the Khecheopalri Lake site.

About 3% and 1% area fall under the wasteland category (rock outcrop and landslide). In the case of the lake area, major changes are recorded in the form of bog area expansion (Table 6.1). In 1963, the bog was 3.4 ha, which increased to 7 ha in 1997 (Jain et al., 2000).

The conversion of dense mixed forest to open mixed forest and then to degraded forests has been mainly attributed to fuelwood and timber extraction, fodder collection and grazing. Agricultural land expansion in the lake watershed had a major impact on the health of the lake through increased sediment deposition.

6.4. Resource Utilization Pattern

Forest-human interaction is an age-old phenomenon that has been crucial for the livelihood of people. The high demand for fuelwood, fodder and timber poses a threat to the forest in the surrounding area. Chopping and lopping of highly preserved tree species for fuelwood, fodder and timber has put tremendous pressure on some selective species. For this, attention was focused on the fuelwood, fodder and timber flows. The magnitudes of these flows are particularly important because they are closely linked and represent the direct removal of biomass from the forests.

6.4.1. Fuelwood Consumption

A consumption rate of 24 kg/day was estimated for each household in the area during 1997-98. Consumption of the commercial alternative source of energy, i.e., kerosene and LPG (14% and 3%, respectively), is insignificant. There is no evidence of non-conventional sources of energy being used by any of the stakeholders. Fuelwood consumption by the different stakeholders is presented in table 6.2. Domestic cooking is the major consumer of fuelwood. Consumption ranges from the maximum of 2264 Mg yr-v by the community to the minimum of 1.02 Mg yr- by pack animal operators. On average, the hotels/lodges consume about 40 to 50 kg of fuelwood per day. A large quantity (240 kg/day/group) of fuelwood is used by HMI during the training period for cooking and other purposes. The porters burn about 2 kg of fuelwood per day during the trek for cooking and water heating.

Annual (394 Mg) fuelwood consumption for water heating and other purposes is low compared to cooking (Table 6.2). When consumption for cooking, water heating, and other purposes is pooled, the fuelwood required is 2264 Mg yr-I by the community, 101 Mg yr-I by hotels/lodges, 45 Mg yr-I by HMI and 26 Mg yr-I by other stakeholders (Table 6.2). Seasonal differences in fuelwood use are attributed to colder weather in winter, followed by the rainy season, and its lowest use is recorded in the summer season (Table 6.3). The annual consumption is thus 1,222, 814, and 400 Mg, respectively, in the winter, rainy, and summer seasons.

The survey indicates that fuelwood is the most important forest product collected (Table 6.2 & Plate 2e) by users. The average household collects about 2433 Mg yr-I in the Yuksam-Dzongri-Goechha La corridor and 1126 Mg yr-I in the Khecheopalri Lake site, or about Rs 3046259 (US$74299) and Rs 1407478 (US$34329) worth of fuelwood per year. The total value of collected fuelwood in both sites is Rs 4535748 (US$110628) yr-I (Table 6.2).

Based on the assumption that the consumption quantity corresponds to the collection quantity, the total fuelwood consumption calculated earlier could be regarded as the demand or pressure on the forests. If the demand per day (7 Mg) is divided by the total area of the trail (3709 ha) and multiplied by 365, the annual pressure is 0.68 Mg of fuelwood on each hectare of forestland. The assumption underlying this calculation is that all the fuelwood required in the area is supplied from the forest alone.

Fuelwood demand by communities and tourism-related activities in the mountains is believed to have a considerable impact on the forests and wildlife (Bjonness, 1980; Byers, 1986; Banskota & Sharma, 1994). The demand for forest wood for fire in the KNP trekking corridor appears to be, at first instance, less (2434 Mg) than the net wood production (21769 Mg). However, the gap between demand and supply is not in fact so small for the following reason. First, the people in the surroundings of the forest area tend to collect fuelwood repeatedly from the same patches of the forestland. The forest cover in close proximity to the settlement and camping sites experiences maximum pressure. As the supply declines nearby, the people walk further and further into the forest, widening the area of the impacted zone. The second factor that has put pressure is the selective use of species of choice for fuel. In recent years, quality fuelwood trees have become sparse. Now, the quality of fuelwood used is poor, and the shortage of good-quality fuelwood has led to widespread switching over to inferior quality fuelwood. The distance covered and the time devoted to fuelwood collection from surrounding forests are widely used indicators of fuelwood scarcity. High pressure was observed in Monastery forest at Dubdi (39%), followed by KNP trail (22%), Goucharan (21%) and trail outside KNP (18%) (Table

6.4). It is apparent that if the harvested quantity exceeds the production capacity, not only will the growing stock be depleted, but also biodiversity. The wood for fuel is derived from live, dead and damaged trees and woody shrubs. The large-scale felling of trees and shrubs along the trek route and campsite is accelerating the degradation process. The forest is depleted, leading to erosion of topsoil and disturbing the ecology of the area. The drudgery associated with fuelwood collection is generally recognized in many parts of India (Guller, 1982; Agarwal, 1989; Sharma, 1993) and other developing countries (Soussan et al., 1991).

The settlements that depend on fuelwood from the KNP corridor and other forests are given in table 6.5. The total consumption of fuelwood is estimated to be 1223 Mg yr-1 in the KNP corridor and 1141 Mg yr-1 in other forests. Thus, the total consumption of fuelwood in and around the KNP is estimated to be 2434 Mg yr. The choice of fuelwood species has now changed from Castanopsis spp. (Katus), and Quercus spp. (Book and Phalant) to Alnus nepalensis (Utish), Engelhardia spicata (Mahuwa), Symplocos theifolia (Kharane), and many shrub species, due to indiscriminate felling of preferred species. At Dzongri, rhododendron bushes are cut for fuel wood purposes. The major impacts on forests are found in the areas of traditional settlements. Forests within about 3 km of Yuksam village have been degraded as a result of fuelwood collection and tree felling. Pairwise ranking of species used as fuelwood along Yuksam-Dzongri Goechella corridor is presented in table 6.6.

6.4.2. Species under Pressure

An inventory of species used for fuelwood at low and high altitudes showed that the trees surrounding the village vicinity, irrespective of species, have the maximum pressure of fuelwood extraction. Nevertheless, certain species are preferred over others for fuel use because of their higher heat output. Quercus lamellosa, Schima wallichi, Eurya acuminata, and Cedrela toona are the most preferred species at low altitudes. At high altitude, Rhododendron spp., Quercus lineata, Quercus lamellosa, Betula alnoides, and Magnolia spp. are the preferred fuelwood species. However, the availability of these preferred species in the forest is under tremendous pressure (Table 6.6). At Tshoka, where a major portion of fuelwood consumers are the Tibetan refugees, tourists, and HMI trainees, form a fairly large portion of fuelwood resource user groups. Still, many species from natural forests, especially

Rhododendron arboreum, R. barbatum, and Magnolia spp., are felled for fuel use.

6.4.3. Fodder Utilization

Animal husbandries in both sites are mainly dependent on the surrounding forests (Plate 2f). This dependence and structured biomass utilization are outlined in table 6.7. These forests are heavily lopped along the trail route and the margins of the settlements. The grazing pressure of cattle and Yaks/Dzos is seasonal and more prominent in the study sites (Plates 3a & 3b). During the past five years, an emphasis has been given to Yak/Dzo rearing. The livestock populations of Yuksam-Dzongri Goechha La corridor increased from 1530 in 1996 to 1708 in 1998. The Yak/Dzo and cattle need about 33 kg of green fodder per day, and a sheep needs about 15 kg per day. Average fodder collection per household is 22 Mg yr-I at both sites. The annual consumption is thus 13092 Mg yr-1 and 2193 Mg yr-1, respectively, in Yuksam and the Khecheopalri Lake site.

The livestock that depend on fodder from the KNP and Lake Site are given in table 6.7. The total consumption of fodder is estimated to be 20728 kg/day in the corridor forests. Pairwise ranking of fodder species along the Yuksam-Dzongri-Goechha La corridor and the Khecheopalri Lake is presented in table 6.8. Nebara, Kanyu, Gagoon, and Dudhilo are the most preferred species because they are highly nutritious. The other species, such as Amliso, Asaray, and Pipli, are less preferred in both sites. A major portion (60%) of the fodder demand is fulfilled mainly by forests, and 40% by agricultural fields.

6.4.4 Timber Utilization

A detailed survey in the surrounding villages of both sites revealed that a large number of woody species are utilized for different purposes, such as for in-house construction and for making agricultural implements (Table 6.9). Nearly 21 different woody species have been listed as highly preferred by the villagers in both sites (Table 6.10). Most of these species are collected from the surrounding forests. Okhar is a highly preferred timber species, but it is not available now because of high extraction. The other preferred species are Chanp, Bajrant and Katus. The least preferred species for timber purposes are Dhuppi and Uttis.

Family fragmentation occurs every 20-25 years, leading mostly to the construction of many new houses, and almost all houses are made of wood. A survey of households in the villages of Yuksam and the Khecheopalri Lake showed that a double-storied building/lodge needs about 600 to 700 ft3 of wood. The Government of Sikkim has restricted the felling of trees for the construction of lodges and houses; however, huge amounts of timber are still being used. Generally, large timber poles are harvested for making ceilings, doors, windows and beams. Medium-sized poles are used for furniture and its repair. Small-sized poles (mainly bamboo) are cut for making cattle sheds or temporary huts (Table 6.9).

Despite the large area of relatively unutilized forests available in both sites, there is ample evidence of long-term degradation. In general, the condition of the forest varies with altitude (distance from the village) and aspects. The forest surrounding the settlements is most degraded. Similar concentric circles of degraded forests surround the villages in other portions of the Indian Himalaya (Pandey & Singh, 1984).

6.4.5 Overland Flow and Soil Loss

Water runoff (% of rainfall) is highest in the trekking corridor (6.57%) and lowest in the alpine pasture (2.44%). Soil loss is also recorded as the greatest in the trekking corridor (Table 6.11 & Plate 3c) in the Yuksam-Dzongri-Goechha La corridor. The runoff is recorded as greatest in wasteland (4.8%) and smallest in cardamom-based agroforestry (.80/0). Soil loss is highest in the cropped area, while it is lowest in the cardamom-based agroforestry system in the Khecheopalri Lake area. The overland flow and the soil loss in the large cardamom-based agroforestry system are less because of good tree canopy and understory thick large cardamom bush coverage. The total soil loss from the lake watershed is 502 Mg km-2 yr-I and soil deposition in the lake is 141 Mg yr-I. The increase in the number of heavily laden pack animals on the trail causes soil erosion.

6.4.6. Solid Waste

Garbage has been an ongoing concern for many years in the Yuksam-Dzongri-Goechha La corridor and the Lake site. Since 1980, KNP regulations have required mountaineering training and trekking groups to pack out their waste, but very few groups have complied. The result has been a continuing accumulation of trash on the route up to Goechha La and HMI base camp and surrounding the sacred lake area. The increasing proliferation of plastics, metals, and glasses has been exacerbated not only by the careless disposal of trash but also by the increased non-biodegradable garbage being generated by the Khanchendzonga Conservation Committee, a village-based NGO. The garbage dumps at base camp have become dangerous (Plate 3d). Tourism waste has continued to be an eyesore along the trekking corridor. Garbage dumps induced by tourism have high visibility and raise immediate concerns from both tourists and the host community. In 1996, the Khanchendzonga Conservation Committee organized a clean-up campaign of the trekking corridor, collecting a huge amount of litter, including 50 kg of plastic bags, 100 kg of empty cans and 100 kg of bottles during the fall season.

6.5. Economic Valuation

6.5.1. Socio-economic Analysis

6.5.1.1. Yuksam-Dzongri-Goechlaa La trekking corridor

The preliminary findings and summary statistics of the samples of 545 respondents are presented in table 6.12. In the case of local community members, the sample has a mean age of 36 years, with respondents ranging from 20 to 55 years of age. More than 90% of the samples consist of male respondents. The mean household size is 5 members and varies from 2 to 9 members. As far as domestic visitors are concerned, the mean age is 33, with respondents ranging from 19 to 65 years of age. The mean age of foreign visitors is 39, ranging from 20 to 67 years. Regarding the educational qualifications of the local communities, 15% of the respondents are illiterate, 23% have less than 10 years of schooling, approximately 34% have obtained a high school diploma, 9% hold a higher secondary diploma, and 9% have a bachelor's degree. The educational qualification of domestic visitors shows that 9% are master's degree holders, 81% are bachelor's degree holders, and

10% have higher secondary education. In the case of foreign visitors, 25% respondents have a master's degree, 60% have a bachelor's degree, and 15% have a higher secondary education. The occupation of local community members shows that 31% of respondents are from the service sector, 32% are from farming and off-farm activities, 21% are from tourism, and 16% are businesspeople. Occupation of domestic and foreign tourists shows that 45% and 40% are in government service, 34% and 51% are professionals, 10% and 6% are in business, 10% and 1% are students, respectively. Small fractions (1 to 2%) of domestic and foreign visitors are retired persons. 34% of the foreign tourists are French and Swedish, 16% are British, 11.1% are German, 5% are American, and 33% are from other countries.

The attractions for visitors are diverse. A majority come for recreation/trekking, followed by those who come to view mountain peaks, wilderness, and birds, as well as specialized interest groups focused on flora and culture.

Trekking duration ranges from 5 to 15 days, with an average of 9 days. Normal daily expenditure by tourists ranges from Rs 190 to Rs 1,710, with an average value of Rs 988, depending on the nature of the trek (independent or organized tourism). In response to their interest on protecting the forest/wildlife of the park, about 23% foreign and 26% domestic tourists are "not interested", 26% foreign and 42% domestic tourists are "fairly interested", 33% foreign and 12% domestic tourists are "interested", and 18% foreign and 20% domestic tourists are "very much interested".

Analysis of visitors' attitude on environment perception towards protection of the KNP reveals that 42% and 59% domestic and foreign visitors consider it "very important", 38% and 32% consider it "important", 12% and 5% consider it "not very important" and 8% and 4% consider it "unimportant", respectively. Perception of biodiversity loss justification in the context of India shows that the majority of both domestic and foreign tourists agree to this point (Table 6.13). A question regarding the direct relevance of KNP for the avoidance of biodiversity loss at any cost is not acceptable to the local community, as it highlights their dependency on natural resources. On the contrary, about 50% of both domestic and foreign tourists agree to the avoidance of biodiversity loss at any cost (Table 6.13).

In response to environmental problems and steps to be taken for conservation, about 10% have said that there is no need to conserve the biodiversity of KNP because it is already in good condition, while 90%

express conservation needs. On the question of who should conserve and maintain the KNP, about 55% are not sure. Among the proposed implementing authorities, the majority of international tourists believe that conservation in the KNP should be a collective effort, with the next most ranked being a joint effort between government and community (Table 6.14). Domestic tourists have responded similarly, desiring the government and community to play the primary role, followed by a collective effort, and then the government (Table 6.14). When asked whether they feel responsible for the maintenance of the Yuksam-Dzongri-Goechha La trek route, 855 of the respondents have given a positive response, whereas 15% have responded negatively.

6.5.1.2. Khecheopalri Lake

The basic statistics of the Khecheopalri Lake site are presented in table 6.15. The average household size is 6 people, and the mean age of the respondents is 43, ranging from 25 to 75 years. Approximately 40% of the community respondents are illiterate, while 45% have received an education up to the secondary level. Of the respondents, 85% are involved in farming-related activities, 13% are in the business/tourism sector, and 2% are in the government sector (Table 6.15).

The mean age of the pilgrims is 43 years, ranging from 22 to 68 years, and the average group size is 8 (Table 6.15). About 20% of the pilgrims are illiterates, 33% have passed secondary education, 31% have passed higher secondary education, and 15% are bachelor's degree holders. The mean monthly income is Rs. 6232 and ranges from 2993 to 13981. The majority (48%) of the pilgrims are government service holders, 31% are farmers, 12% are business people, and 9% are students.

For domestic visitors, the mean age is 33 years, ranging from 19 to 65 years. The average family size is 4. About 21% of the domestic visitors have received higher secondary education, 67% have a bachelor's degree, and the remaining 12% have a master's degree. The average monthly income of domestic visitors is Rs. 6724. The majority (78%) of the respondents are from the government sector, followed by 18% business people and 4% students.

The average age of foreign visitors is 34 years, ranging from 20 to 60 years. The majority of the foreign visitors are free and independent trekkers (FITs). The mean monthly income is Rs. 65969. About 72% of the foreign visitors are bachelor's degree holders, 16% are master's degree holders, and 12% have higher secondary education. About 53% are engaged in professional occupations, 29% are in the government sector, 11% are students, and 3% are retired personnel. Total expenditure by the pilgrims at the Lake site (including travel, food, and accommodation) varies from Rs. 164 to 1474 per visit per group (Figure 6.2). The maximum expenditure is by north zone visitors, and the least by those from the west zone.

About 78% of the pilgrims visit the lake for religious purposes, while the majority (85%) of the domestic visitors come for recreation. Most (65%) of the foreign visitors come to the Lake for recreation, while 19% come for religious purposes, and 16% have cited the rich biodiversity of the area as their purpose in visiting.

Approximately 56% of foreign visitors, 43% domestic visitors, 35% of local community members, and 28% of pilgrims have shown some interest in conservation and maintenance of the Lake and its surrounding watersheds. Approximately 53% of domestic visitors, 50% of pilgrims, 45% of community members and 37% of foreign visitors feel that the state govermnent should take initiation for conserving the Lake watershed, whereas 26% of the local community, 22% of local pilgrims, 20% of domestic and 6% of foreign visitors feel that the village level institutions, in this case the panchayat (village council), should have this responsibility.

6.5.2 Recreational/Sacredness Value

Across all zones, travel cost for local pilgrims is positively related to visitation rate. Assuming that each zone represents a single average travel cost and opportunity cost of time, a TC model has been used to calculate the consumer surplus (Table 6.16). A demand curve has been prepared by evaluating the travel expenditures that visitors are willing to make to visit the Lake. Multiple regression analysis has been carried out to estimate the parameters of the linear travel cost demand equation.

The coefficients of the first and second equations are statistically significant (Table 6.17). In the second equation, the t-values of both variables are statistically significant ($P< 0.01$, $P<0.05$), although the adjusted R2 value is low because only one independent variable is considered (Table 6.17). The adjusted R2 value of the first equation is higher than that of the first, but the t-value of the distance is not significant. We have attempted to develop other equations that include all the variables: travel cost (T), distance (D), income (INC), age (AGE), density (DEN), and literacy (LIT).

However, these equations are not considered because the coefficients are not statistically significant. In fact, the Khecheopalri Lake is a place of religious importance; therefore, literacy, age, distance and income do not play an important role in visiting the site. The lending rate of interest of the Reserve Bank of India was 10% during 1997-98. The inflation rate showed fluctuations during the year; however, the average annual rate of inflation was estimated to be 4.83%. Therefore, the real rate of interest was 5.17%. The present sacredness values are presented in table 6.18. The estimated consumer surplus for visits to the Khecheopalri Lake is US$661 and US$1562 from the first and second consumer surplus, respectively (Table 6.16). Recreational/ Sacredness value per visitor is US$3.87 as calculated from the consumer surplus. The total number of local pilgrims to the Khecheopalri Lake was 7800 in 1998, and the aggregate annual recreational/sacredness value amounted to US$30186 for pilgrims. The higher cost of travel and the distance of the Lake from various zones have restricted the visitation rate by pilgrims. The west zone is the closest and exhibits the minimum travel cost, as the Lake is located in this zone, where the highest visitation rate is recorded (Figure 6.3).

Time spent by visitors on worship, viewing and photography of the Lake site is 27% of the total. Assuming a constant sacredness value of time for all activities, the sacredness value of the Khecheopalri Lake viewing is estimated to be US$2378 per annum.

The demand curve function for recreational value shows that the probability of visitation increases with decreasing travel cost and distance for local pilgrims (within Sikkim visitors). The consumer surplus of Khecheopalri Lake is relatively low compared to ecotourism demand in Madagascar (Mallie & Mendelsohn, 1993) and the economic value of elephant viewing in Kenya (Brown & Henry, 1989), primarily due to the low visitation rate. However, the sacredness value of the Lake site is fairly intact, and consequently, the biodiversity and recreation values have also remained high. An expected growth in tourism may increase the consumer surplus, but this may be at the cost of the aesthetic, biodiversity and religious value of the Lake site. Therefore, a balance between consumer surplus and other values for conservation and preservation has ultimately to be established. The results of the present study are very similar to those from some other sites in tropical India, especially on a protected area at a tiger reserve in Kerala and a national park in Bharatpur that show low values (Chopra et al., 1997;

Manoharan et al., 1998). However, the present value for the Lake site is higher, despite its low visitation rate and lack of protection compared to the above two destinations.

6.5.3. Analyzing Willingness-to-Pay

Generally, those respondents who are getting direct benefits from the park have been considered for the analysis of WTP, but in the present study, the WTP is assumed to be a function of the respondents' personal characteristics and income level. Another variable, education level, has been used as an explanatory variable. A greater number of years of schooling would arguably increase the knowledge of a person. Perhaps education would help a person better comprehend the environmental effects of economic development. Age and gender have also been used as explanatory variables. Results of both sites of the willingness-to-pay (WTP) exercise, for community members, pilgrims, resident visitors and non-resident visitors are presented in tables 6.19 and 6.20. The result shows that the average response rate for the Yuksam-Dzongri-Goechha La corridor is 45%, on the question regarding the motivation behind respondents' WTP for conservation. Only 31 local community members have indicated a willingness to pay for better management of the KNP. Approximately 25 community members have stated that they are willing to pay, but due to financial constraints and other responsibilities, they are unable to do so at this time. 30 community members have indicated willingness to perform voluntary work by providing manual labour for trail maintenance and cleanup. Respondents who are willing to volunteer have agreed to set aside about a day per month. Some of them have said that they can provide seedlings for plantations in the surrounding areas. Nine community members have refused completely to pay in kind or in cash for conservation. In case of foreign tourists, only 49% have indicated a positive reaction to WTP for conservation, while 27% have agreed on condition that the amount would be utilized in a constructive manner, and 24% have refused to pay. In the case of domestic tourists, about 60% respondents have shown an indifferent attitude towards paying for conservation because they feel that it is the responsibility of the state government and local communities.

An analysis of the WTP provides an opportunity to study the content and context validity of the interview schedule. An Ordinary Least Squares (OLS) regression has been used to analyze WTP. The regression reveals that the variables have attained the expected signs, as presented in table 6.21. The

R2 value is encouraging in the present context. Age shows a positive correlation with WTP in the case of all domestic, foreign visitors, and local communities. It is found that the middle-aged and older age group of people can spare the money to accept CV bids, while the young age group can spare less. This suggests that age is a significant factor for all types of respondents in accepting the SWTP.

Educational qualification does not show a significant correlation with WTP when zero bid is included; however, on exclusion of "refuse the bids", it shows a positive correlation with WTP (P< 0.003). This is mainly attributed to less educated respondents opting for most of the "refused the bids" for WTP. Fifty-five per cent of the total responses are "refuse to pay". Occupation is not a major factor in accepting the CV bids. Those people who are directly involved with tourism-related activities and get more economic returns are interested in paying for WTP as compared to those who do not get the economic benefits from tourism. The results also indicate that businessmen are willing to pay more than professionals. This finding has important policy implications as businessmen have the most potential for financing environmental improvements. Sex also does not influence the visitation rate and WTP for conservation. The income of visitors significantly influences their WTP for conservation of the area (Table 6.21). For the entire sample, using means of variables, the estimated willingness to pay for the management of the KNP is US$8.84 by foreign visitors per trip, US$1.91 by domestic visitors per trip, and US$6.20 by the local community on an annual basis. This indicates that foreign visitors place higher recreational/conservation values on the experience than do domestic visitors and local community members.

The question regarding confidentiality concerns the right amount for their conservation contribution, with 26% of local community members, 22% of domestic, and 20% of international contributions. Foreign visitors have stated that they are "very confident", while 55%, 52% and 40% are "confident", respectively. About 13% local community members, 16% domestic, and 28% foreign visitors are "undecided"; the remaining are "not very confident". These responses suggest that the amounts stated by the respondents are valid.

The response rates for the Khecheopalri Lake against WTP are highest for the foreign visitors (68%), followed by pilgrims (54%), community members (40%) and domestic visitors (36%) (Table 6.20). The regression reveals that the variables have attained the expected signs as presented in table 6.22. The age of the interviewer shows a positive correlation with WTP for all visitors and also among local community members. It is found that the middle-aged and older age group can spare the money to accept CV bids, while the young age group spends less. Thus, the age of the people is a major factor for all types of respondents in WTP. Sex does not influence the visitation rate and WTP for conservation. Occupation, education and income of the visitors significantly influence their WTP for conservation of the area (Table 6.22). Multiple R is very encouraging, and so are the F-statistics. For the entire sample, using means of variables, the estimated annual WTP for the management of the Khecheopalri Lake is US$0.88 for local community members per year, and US$2.16 for local pilgrims, US$2.51 for domestic visitors, and US$7.19 for foreign visitors per visit (Table 6. 22).

Compared to other parts of India, the frequency of visitors is less at both sites because most visitors seldom return to trek in the same area a second time. Therefore, the WTP stated by all the visitors is for that particular trek, while a small number of foreign tourists have stated that they would like to help voluntary organizations for community and environmental development in the host region. This study reveals that the visitors' WTP does not depend on the benefits they would receive from preserving the sites, but most of them have stated that their WTP is primarily to maintain the beautiful, unexploited landscape and rich biodiversity of these areas. The demand for nature/ecotourism in Sikkim by foreign and domestic visitors has also been increasing enormously. Walsh (1986) gave an overview of the price elasticity of demand for various recreational activities. The price elasticity of demand for a recreational activity is generally low when the proportion of income spent on it is low (Walsh, 1986). This may be an indication of the income effect at the national income level. As respondents' income levels grow, the income elasticity may improve for environmental goods. The probability of participation increases with age and increasing income. The magnitude of economic problems restricts domestic visitors from visiting the trekking corridor because the entry fees for the park are relatively high compared to other protected areas. Therefore, visits to the KNP are given low priority by most of the domestic tourists, except for a few rich individuals and people from India's West Bengal, Maharashtra, Delhi and Gujarat. WTP for all categories of visitors and the local community shows significant co-variance. The WTP is significantly related to age, education and income levels. The findings of this study are similar to those of Walsh (1986), where age and income appeared to be the most important socio-economic variables determining the probability of participation in recreation activity. This was expected, as an increase in income level would show respondents' greater willingness to spend on recreation.

Sex does not significantly influence the WTP. The WTP per trip is significantly higher for foreign tourists than for domestic ones, which is mainly attributed to higher income levels and greater environmental awareness. Local residents' WTP for the entire year is no less significant for this group, which has a long-term stake in the area. Aspects of time, services, or traded goods (tree seedlings in the present study), contributed by the local community, are of no less value than WTP. Therefore, contributions by those who are willing to give time and materials for environmental conservation should be a part of WTP. A quantification methodology for this needs to be developed in future studies. Extrapolating to the Yuksam Dzongri-Goechha La corridor and the sacred Khecheopalri Lake, using total visitors and community households, the annual WTP of US$8,777 and US$46,940 for maintenance and preservation appears significant. The application of TCM and WTP strongly supports the enterprise-based community involved in biodiversity/nature conservation, and suggests that the concept of ecotourism has permeated all levels of direct and indirect beneficiaries/stakeholders.

6.6. Conclusion

Dependence on fuelwood for energy is causing serious deforestation problems in the trekking corridor and the Lake site. The pressure is far greater in Monastery forest than in the trail forest outside the Khangchendzonga National Park. The consumption of fuelwood varies amongst stakeholders with respect to different physical and economic factors, causing serious deforestation problems in the trail and the Lake site. The widespread switching over to inferior quality of fuelwood species is an indicator of pressure in the forests of both sites. Fuelwood continues to be the primary source of cooking in the trekking corridor, while commercial alternative energy sources contribute very little. Enhancing the supply of fuelwood through plantations and reducing the fuelwood demand through providing an alternative source of energy can facilitate this.

A contingent valuation method has been used to estimate the willingness-to-pay (WTP) for conservation and protection of natural resources in the sites. The results indicate a strong positive response. The survey has received a positive response from local communities, pilgrims, residents, and non-resident visitors, demonstrating their willingness to conserve the area. The analysis reports that the mean WTP per visitor per visit is higher for non-resident visitors than for resident visitors. Local community members are willing to pay for environmental management. The multiple regression on WTP reveals that the attitudes of respondents, their visitation rate, and the number of aspects of the area they consider valuable are important determinants of WTP for the trekking corridor and the Lake site. Variables have attained the expected sign, and they are statistically significant and encouraging for a small study such as the present one.

The CVM may also be useful in providing more relevant information for decision-makers for investment and policy purposes. The study results are very encouraging for trail and lake management. It proves that the local people, as well as visitors, are aware of the environmental damage caused by the increasing visitation rate and the overexploitation of the natural resources of the area and its importance. It is also clear that the willingness-to-pay in terms of cash or kind exists for contributing towards the upkeep and improvement of the trail and the lake.

The lake has recreational and biodiversity values for domestic and foreign visitors, and more sacredness values for the Sikkimese. The demand curve function for recreation increases with a decrease in travel cost and distance for the Sikkimese. The lake has demonstrated high recreational/sacredness values, which are attributed to the conservation of the site for biodiversity and pilgrims.

The study shows that the Travel Cost (TC) and the Contingent Valuation (CV) methods can be successfully applied to evaluate natural resources of the Hindu-Kush Himalayan region. The results of the study suggest that both sites have an economic potential far greater than their realized economic earnings. Therefore, TCM and CVM can be a useful tool in providing more relevant information for decision-makers for investment and policy purposes in biodiversity hotspots and protected area management.

Land-use / Cover	Yuksam-Dzongri-Goechha La Corridor		Khecheopalri Lake	
	ha	%	ha	%
Forest				
Dense mixed forest	689	18	272.20	22.53
Open mixed forest	720	19	492.01	40.69
Degraded forest	1289	35	254.00	21.00
Rhododendron	30	1	-	-
Alpine Scrub	40	1	-	-
Forest blank	100	3	-	-
Settlement and cultivated area	598	16	162.50	13.44
Rock out crop	45	1	17.50	1.45
Land slide area	58	2	-	-
Water surface (river & lakes)	140	4	3.79	0.31
Bog area	-	-	7.01	0.58
Total	3709	100	1209.00	100

Table 6.1: Area under Different Land-Use/Cover Categories in Yuksam-Dzongrigoechhala Trekking Corridor and Sacred Khecheopalri Lake Site in 1997

Stakeholders	Purpose				Cost (Rs)
	Cooking (Mg yr^{-1})	Water-heating (Mg yr^{-1})	Other (Mg yr^{-1})	Total (Mg yr^{-1})	
Yuksam-Dzongri-Goechha La corridor					
Community	1896	260	109	2264	2829984
Hotel/Lodges	86	12	3	101	126239
HMI	37	6	2	45	56252
Travel Agents	6	1	0.2	7.2	8979
FIT's	1.4	0.3	0.2	1.9	2378
Pack-animal operator	0.8	0.08	0.1	0.98	1230
Porter	13	0.6	2	15.6	19516
Total	2040	280	116	2437	3046259
Khecheopalri lake					
Community	563	737	335	670	837507
Trekker's hut/ Teashops	392	502	137	456	569982
Total	955	1239	472	1126	1407489

Table 6.2: Fuelwood Consumption for Different Purposes by Stakeholders and Its Economic Costs

Stakeholders	Consumption (Mg)				
	Summer (61days)	Rainy (122 days)	Winter (182 days)	Average (Mg d^{-1})	Annual (Mg y^{-1})
Yuksam-Dzongri-Goechha La corridor					
Community	378.32	756.64	1128.76	6.20 [1]	2263.72
Hotel/lodges	16.72	33.45	49.90	0.27 [2]	100.07
HMI	2.30	13.07	28.51	0.24 [3]	43.88
Travel agent	0.16	3.40	3.56	0.010 [4]	7.12
FIT's	0.65	-0.0	1.30	0. 001 [5]	1.95
Pack-animal operator	0.086	0.41	0.53	0.002 [6]	1.026
Porter	0.28	6.25	8.85	0.002 [7]	15.38
Khecheoaplri lake					
Community	111.99	223.99	334.15	0.67	670.14
Trekker's hut/ Tea shops	7.625	15.25	22.75	0.046	45.62

1, 2: Community and hotel consumption per day; 3, 4: Per group; 5, 6, 7: per person

Table 6.3: Stakeholder Wise Seasonal Fuelwood Consumption Pattern

Forest	Household number	User's population	Consumption Pattern		
			Kg d^{-1}	Kg hh^{-1} d^{-1}	Mg yr^{-1}
Yuksam-Dzongri-Goechha La Corridor					
KNP trail	58	331	1432	24.68	522
Trail outside KNP	52	306	1188	22.86	434
Monastry forest at Dubdi	107	610	2517	23.52	919
Goucharan	57	325	1341	23.52	489
Khecheopalri area					
Lake surrounding forest	47	282	1213	25.80	443
Other forest	25	160	630	25.20	230

Table 6.4: Dependency Pattern of Local Community on Trekking Corridor and Lake Surrounding Forests

Settlements	Consumption		
	Kg d^{-1}	Kg $capita^{-1}$ d^{-1}	Mg yr^{-1}
Yuksam-Dzongri-Goechha La corridor			
Dependent on corridor forest			
Tshoka (inside KNP)	250	4.39	91
Geychen	422	3.52	154
Norbugang	494	4.05	180
Khongtay	893	3.69	326
Yuksam	1292	4.41	472
Total	3351	3.87	1223
Dependent on other forest			
Kopchey	282	4.21	103
Mantabong	518	3.75	189
Tshong	988	5.77	360
Topsing	494	3.66	180
Gufa Danra	141	4.03	52
Dostang	'282	3.62	103
Mangsabong	424	3.71	154
Total	3129	4.10	1141
All Settlements (corridor)	6480	4.73	2364
Khecheopalri lake			
Khecheopalri	403	4.2	147
Chojo & Golai	1557	4.5	568
All Settlements (Khecheopalri lake)	1960	4.3	715

Table 6.5: Settlement Wise Fuelwood Consumption Pattern in the Study Sites

Species (local name)	Yuksam-Dzongri-Goechha La Corridor		Khecheopalri Lake	
	Preferred	Available	Preferred	Available
Abies densa (Gobre salla)	4	9	-	-
Acer oblongum (Phirphire)	4	4	-	-
Acer papilio (Kapase)	3	4	-	-
Albizzia procera (Seris)	-	-	7	0
Alnus nepalensis (Uttis)	2	11	0	1
Arundenaria sp. (Parang)	6	1	-	-
Beilschmiedia sikkimensis (Tarsing)	7	5	-	-
Betula alnoides (Saur)	8	3	-	-
Castonopsis hystrix (Jat katus)	4	10	9	10
Cedrela toona (Tooni)	6	2	-	-
Cryptomeria japonica (Dhuppi)	2	2	-	-
Dendrocalamus sp. (Bans)	1	3	9	4
Edgeworthia gardeneri (Argeli)	-	-	4	12
Engelhardtia spicata (Mahuwa)	-	-	7	6
Eurya acuminata (Jhinguni)	8	8	13	7
Litsaea elongata (Pahenli)	2	4	-	-
Magnolia campbellii (Ghonge chanp)	6	5	-	-
Magnolia sp. (Phurse chanp)	6	7	-	-
Machilus sp. (Chanp)	-	-	7	2
Michilus edulis (Phumse)	-	-	6	10
Prunus cerasoides (Panyun)	5	1	-	-
Prunus nepaalensis (Arupate)	2	4	-	-
Quercus lamellosa (Bajrant)	10	8	-	-
Qurcus linesata (Phalant)	11	3	-	-
Rhododendron arboreum (Lali guras)	6	10	-	-
R . barbatum (Curling)	6	4	-	-
R . falconeri (Curling)	4	14	-	-
Rhus insignis *(Bhalayo)*	-	-	3	12
R . semialata *(Bhakimlo)*	-	-	3	7
Schima wallichii *(Chilauney)*	9	2	-	-
Sorbus sp. (Pansi)	2	2	-	-
Symplocos ramosissima (Kharane)	1	1	10	10
Viburnum codyfolium (Asare)	5	7	11	6

* Availability for species were assigned as per their abundance at the designated plots. Higher the scores, more abundance are the species.

Table 6.6: Pair-wise Ranking of Species Used as Fuelwood in Both the Sites Viburnum Codyfolium (Asare)

Livestock	Number		Consumption			
			(kg d^{-1})		(Mg yr^{-1})	
	Yuksam	Khecheopalri	Sites			
			Yuksam	Khecheopalri	Yuksam	Khecheopalri
Cattle	454	110	13620	3300	4971	1204
Goat	311	106	4665	1590	1703	580
Sheep	461	22	6915	330	2524	120
Pig	260	66	3120	792	1139	289
Dzo	122	-	4270	-	1558	-
Yak	78	-	2730	-	996	-
Horse	22	-	550	-	201	-

Table 6.7: Fodder Consumption Rate of Different Livestock in the Study Sites

Species (local name)	Yuksam-Dzongri-Goechha La Corridor		Khecheopalri lake	
	Preferred	Available	Preferred	Available
Acer oblongum (Phirphire)	1	2	-	2
Acer papilio (Kapase)	1	6	-	8
Aconogonum molle (Thotne)	-	-	6	14
Albizzia procera (Siris)	-	-	8	4
Artemesia vulgaris (Teteypaty)	9	13	1	12
Arundinaria sp. (Parang)	9	3	14	8
Beilschmiedia sikkimensis (Tarsing)	17	15	-	-
Betula alnoides (Saur)	3	6	-	-
Bassaiopsis mitis (Phutta)	-	-	21	10
Cedrela toona (Tooni)	6	1	20	6
Cyperus sp. (Bukki)	7	3	-	-
Dendrocalamus sp. (Bans)	8	4	14	12
Elastosima sessile (Gagleto)	14	17	7	20
Engelhardtia spicata (Mahuwa)	-	-	4	10
Eragrostis tenella (Banso)	16	12	-	-

Ficus nemoralis (Dudhilo)	19	11	19	8
Ficus roxburghii (Nebera)	22	20	25	17
Ficus foereslata (Dudhe lahara)	-	-	23	11
Koelaria cristata (Seeru)	10	13	-	-
Litsaea citrata (Siltimur)	-	-	14	6
Litsaea elongata (Pahenli)	10	4	-	-
Macaranga pustulata (Malata)	-	-	13	10
Machilus edulis (Phunse)	-	-	7	20
Magnolia sp. (Phusre chanp)	1	8	-	-
Pauzolzia viminea (Chiple)	15	14	13	23
Paveta indica (Kanyu)	21	2	-	-

Ficus nemoralis (Dudhilo)	19	11	19	8
Ficus roxburghii (Nebera)	22	20	25	17
Ficus foereslata (Dudhe lahara)	-	-	23	11
Koelaria cristata (Seeru)	10	13	-	-
Litsaea citrata (Siltimur)	-	-	14	6
Litsaea elongata (Pahenli)	10	4	-	-
Macaranga pustulata (Malata)	-	-	13	10
Machilus edulis (Phunse)	-	-	7	20
Magnolia sp. (Phusre chanp)	1	8	-	-
Pauzolzia viminea (Chiple)	15	14	13	23
Paveta indica (Kanyu)	21	2	-	-

Prunus cerosoides (Panyun)	3	20	14	-
Prunus rufa (Lekh panyun)	4	2	-	-
Pentapanax leschenaultii (Chinde)	-	-	2	-
Quercus lamellosa (Bajrant)	4	6	-	-
Rhaphidophora sp. (Kanchirna)	-	-	22	8
Saurauia nepaulensis (Gagoon)	20	9	23	14
Symingtonia populnea (Pipli)	2	9	4	-
Symplocos ramosissima (Kharane)	1	1	-	23
Thysanlaena maxima (Amliso)	17	18	17	18
Viburnum cordifolium (Asare)	1	18	3	20

* Availability for species were assigned as per their abundance at the designated plots. Higher the scores, more abundance are the species.

Table 6.8: Pair-wise Ranking of Preferred and Available Species of Fodder in Study Sites

Large size poles	
Time interval (years)	15 – 25
Tree number	2 - 5
Average (DBH) size	20 – 40 cm
Wood volume required	2.35 – 4.77 m^3
Medium size poles)	
Time interval (years)	5 – 7
Tree number	10 – 15
Average size (DBH) size	10 – 20 cm
Wood volume required	2.16 – 7.1 m^3
Small size poles (mainly bamboo)	
Time intervals (years)	3 – 5 years
Number of poles required	80 – 120
Average(DBH) size	< 10 cm

Table 6.9: Other Uses of Forest Products
(House Construction and Maintenance) for an Average Household

Species (local name)	Yuksam-Dzongri-Goechha La corridor		Khecheopalri Lake	
	Preferred	Available	Preferred	Available
Abies densa (Gobre salla)	11	12	-	-
Acer laevigatum (Putli)	4	1	-	-
Acer oblongum (Phirphire)	8	3	-	-
Albizzia procera (Siris)	-	-	5	10
Alnus nepalensis (Uttis)	1	11	10	3
Beilschmiedia sikkimensis (Tarsing)	2	5	12	2
Betula alnoides (Saur)	8	11	10	8
Castonopsis hystrix (Jat katus)	7	8	11	12
Cedrela toona (Tooni)	7	4	6	6
Dendrocalamus spp (Bans)	1	9	-	-
Elaeocarpus lanceaefolius (Bhadrase)	-	-	7	7
Engelhardtia spicata (Mahuwa)	-	-	7	0
Juglans regia (Okhar)	11	2	9	12
Machilus *sp. (Bhaise kawlo)*	-	-	13	5
Machilus edulis *(Phunse)*	5	8	11	9
Machilus odoratissima (Lali kaula)	5	2	-	-
Magnolia campbellii (Ghoge champ)	4	13	-	-
Michelia exelsa (Rani champ)	10	2	2	14
Michelia sp. (Bhalay champ)	-	-	1	12
Prunus nepaulensis (Arupate)	3	5	-	-
Quercus lamellosa (Bajrant)	16	14	3	13
Quercus lineata (Phalant)	8	4	-	-
Rhaphidophora sp (Kanchirna)	6	5	-	-
Schima wallichii (Chilaune)	6	2	7	7
Spondias axillaris (Lapsi)			-	-
Symingtonia populnea (Pipli)	8	9	15	13
Weigtia gigantia (Bauni kat)	2	3	-	-

- Availability for species was assigned as per their abundance at the designated plots. Higher the scores, more abundance are the species.

Table 6.10: Pair-Wise Ranking of Preferred and Available Species of Timber in Study Sites

Land-use	Yuksam – Dzongri – Goechha La Corridor		Khecheopalri Lake	
	Overland flow (% of precipitation)	Soil loss (Kg ha^{-1})	Overland Flow (% of precipitation)	Soil loss (Kg ha^{-1})
Maize field	5.15	335.56	3.79	405
Cardamom field	2.27	49.41	1.79	15
Wasteland	3.15	88.34	4.77	156
Trail corridor	6.57	661.81	-	-
Forest cover	3.46	105.82	2.06	25
Alpine Pasture land	2.44	41.90	-	-

Table 6.11: Overland Flow and Soil Loss of Different Land Use/Cover from the Study Sites

Respondents	Variables					
	AGE	SEX	EDQ	OCU	INC ($)	WTP ($)
Foreign Visitors						
Mean	38.96	1.41	15.11	4.25	4011	8.84
Std. Dev	11.73	0.49	1.50	0.82	4281	11.94
Domestic Visitors						
Mean	32.71	1.18	14.90	4.01	159	1.91
Std. Dev	8.29	0.38	1.12	1.23	66	4.05
Local Community						
Mean	36.20	1.09	8.53	3.19	832	6.20
Std. Dev	8.67	0.29	4.76	1.42	375	19.08

Table 6.12: Basic Statistics of Important Variables in Yuksam-Dzongri-Goechha La Trekking Corridor

AGE: Respondent's age in years; SEX: Male—1, Female—2;

EDQ: Year of schooling; INC: Income (Households' annual income for local community and monthly for visitors);

OCU: Occupation; Service—5, Professional—4, Business—3, retired—2 and student—1 for visitors and Tourism Involved—5, Service—4, Business—3, Labourer—2, and Agriculture—1for community members;

WTP: Willingness to Pay (per trip for visitors and annually for local community).

Opinion	Respondents	Questions	
		Biodiversity loss justification in the context of India	Avoidance of KNP biodiversity loss at any cost
Strongly disagreed	LC	-	28
	DT	3	2
	IT	1	2
Disagreed	LC	-	40
	DT	4	24
	IT	1	28
Neutral	LC	-	17
	DT	19	19
	IT	22	13
Agreed	LC	-	13
	DT	64	48
	IT	63	50
Strongly agreed	LC	-	2
	DT	10	7
	IT	13	7

LC = local community; DT = domestic tourist; IT = International tourist
(-) This question was not asked to the local community

Table 6.13: Respondents' Perception on the Importance of Environmental Issues (%) in Yuksam-Dzongri-Goechha La Trekking Corridor
LC = Local Community; DT = Domestic Tourist; IT = International Tourist (-) This Question Was Not Asked to the Local Community

Implementing authority	Visitors			
	International		Domestic	
	Number	(%)	Number	(%)
Government	38	12	19	15
Non-Government Organization (NGO)	10	3	9	7
Local Community	10	3	12	10
Government and Community	123	38	49	39
Collective effort*	142	43	30	24
Can't Say	2	1	6	5

*Includes visitors, local community, travel operators, NGOs, and government

Table 6.14: Respondents' Attitude for the Protection of Yuksam Dzongri-Goechha La Trekking Corridor

Respondents	Variables					
	AGE	SEX	EDQ	OCU	INC ($)	WTP ($)
Local Community						
Mean	43.42	1.26	5.38	2.08	415.39	0.88
Standard deviation	13.25	0.44	4.39	1.48	392.83	1.57
Local Pilgrims						
Mean	42.67	1.32	10.39	3.80	152.43	2.16
Standard deviation	11.84	0.46	5.09	1.43	68.26	3.50
Domestic Tourist						
Mean	33.04	1.18	14.85	4.10	163.54	2.51
Standard deviation	8.61	0.39	1.13	1.16	67.32	4.48
Foreign Tourist						
Mean	33.84	1.38	14.44	4.25	1608.88	7.19
Standard deviation	9.59	0.49	1.73	1.05	563.31	8.94

Table 6.15: Basic Statistics of Important Variables in Khecheopalri Lake Local Community

AGE: Respondents' age in years;
SEX: Male—1, Female—2;
EDQ: Year of Schooling;
INC: Income (households' annual income for local community and monthly for visitors);

OCU: Occupation; Service—5, Professional—4, Business—3 Retired—2, and Student—1 for visitors and Tourism Involved—5, Service—4, Business—3, Labourer—2, and Agriculture—1 for community members;

WTP: Willingness to pay (per trip for visitors and annually for local community).

Zone (within Sikkim)	Visitation Rate	Travel Cost	Mean Distance	Density	Literacy	Sacredness Value Consumer Surplus (US$)*	
	(%)	(US$)*	(km)	(km^2)	(%)	CS1	CS2
North	23	9.14	225	75	42	12	173
East	29	5.85	129	388	54	109	308
South	32	3.90	72	239	44	189	417
West	45	1.82	55	235	37	351	664
Total	-	-	-	-	-	661	1562

CS = Consumer Surplus,

Table 6.16: Zone Wise Sacredness Value of the Khecheopalri Lake by the Local Sikkimese Pilgrimage Calculated at 1 US$= Rs. 41/- (Average Conversion Rate Calculated for the Year 1998)
CS 1 Calculated Based on Travel Cost and Distance, and CS2 Calculated Based on Travel Cost Only.

Equation Number	Travel Cost Model	Estimated equation	R^2	P-value
I	V = (T, D)	V = 47.959 – 0.184T + 0.196D	0.997	0.03
II	V = (T)	V = 46.988 – 0.069 T	0.845	0.05

Table 6.17: Functional Characteristics or Travel Cost Demand Curve for Valuing Sacredness of the Khecheopalri Lake
V = Visitation Rate, T = Travel Cost, D = Distance

Travel cost model	Total value for 1998	Present value per person	
	($Rs \times 10^3$)	(US$.)*	(Rs.)
V = f (T, D)	380	1.19	49
V = f (T)	910	2.85	117

Table 6.18: Present Sacredness Value of the Khecheopalri Lake by Local Pilgrims Based on the Travel Cost Method

V = Visitation Rate, T= Travel Cost and D= Distance

**Calculated at 1 US$= Rs. 411- (Average conversion rate calculated for the year 1998)*

Variables	WTP		
	Foreign visitors	Domestic visitors	Local community
Mean value per visitor (US$)	8.84	1.91	6.20
**Aggregate value for all visitors (US$.)	5852	1226	1699
*Respondents with WTP (%)	50	40	33
+Response rate (%)	49	19	35

Table 6.19: Summary Results from the Contingent Valuation (CV) Question from Yuksam-Dzongri-Goechha La Trekking Corridor. WTP: Willingness to Pay, US$ 1 = Rs.38/- (As Per the Conversion Rate in 1997)

*** The non-respondents were assumed to have a WTP equal to those that answered*

**Based on total respondents who responded positively for WTP*

+ Based on total visitors/ households

Variables	WTP			
	LC	LP	DT	IT
Mean value per respondents (US$)*	0.88	2.16	2.51	7.19
Aggregate value for all respondents (US$)**	63	16848	25943	4149
Respondents with WTP (%) +	40	54	36	68
Response rate (%) #	69	76	59	80

Table 6.20: Summary result from the Contingent Valuation in the Khecheopalri Lake

LC = Local Community, LP = Local Pilgrims, DT = Domestic Tourist, IT = International Tourist, WTP = Willingness-to-pay

**Calculated at 1US$ = Rs. 41/- (Average conversion rate calculated for the year 1998).*

*** The non-respondents were assumed to have a WTP equal to those that answered*

N

+ Based on total respondents who responded positively for WTP
 # Based on sampled visitors/ households

Components	
Dependent Variables	WTP
No. of observation	243
Multiple R	0.348
Squared multiple R	0.121
Adjusted squared multiple R	0.103
Standard error	489.155

Variables	Coefficient	Std. Error	t value	P<
AGE	9.534	2.860	3.334	0.001
SEX	-41.927	68.196	-0.615	0.539
EDQ	34.167	11.195	3.052	0.003
OCU	-6.886	31.567	-0.218	0.828
INC	0.005	0.002	3.148	0.002

Analysis of variance

	Sum-of-squares	DF	Mean-Squares	F-Ratio	P<
Regression	7828703.690	5	1565740.738	6.544	0.000
Residual	5.67075E+07	237	239272.254		

Table 6.21: Result of Multiple Regression Estimation in Yuksam-Dzongri-Goechha La Trekking Corridor
GE= Age, SEX= Sex, EDQ= Educational Qualification,
OCU=Occupation, INC= Income

Components	
Dependent Variable	WTP
Number of observation	360
Multiple R	0.492
Squared multiple R	0.242
Adjusted squared multiple R	0.231
Standard error of estimate	4.683

Variables	Coefficient	Std. Error	t-value	P (2 Tail)
AGE	0.092	0.024	3.762	0.000
SEX	-0.349	0.545	-0.641	0.522
EDQ	0.228	0.062	3.702	0.000
OCU	-0.290	0.147	-1.974	0.049
INC	0.003	0.000	8.118	0.000

Analysis of Variance

Source	Sum-of-squares	DF	Mean-square	F-ratio	P <
Regression	2474.004	5	494.801	22.56	0.000
Residual	7763.96	354	21.932		

Table 6.22: Result of Multiple Regression Estimation in the Khecheopalri Lake
AGE: Age of the Respondent, Sex: Gender, EDQ: Educational Qualification, OCU: Occupation, INC: Income, WTP: Willingness to Pay Travel Cost

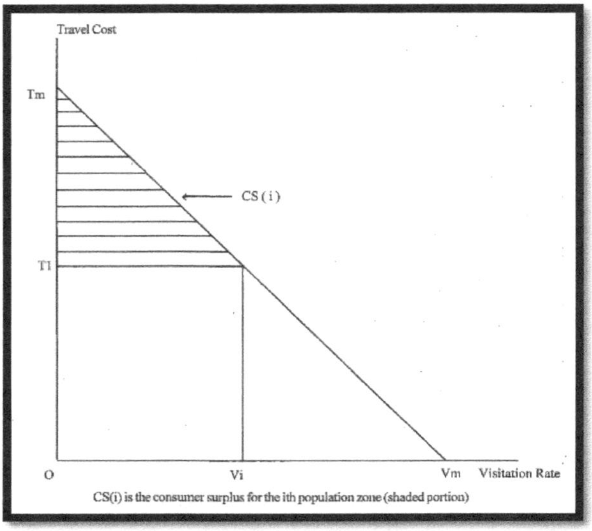

Figure 6.1: Travel Cost Demand Curve

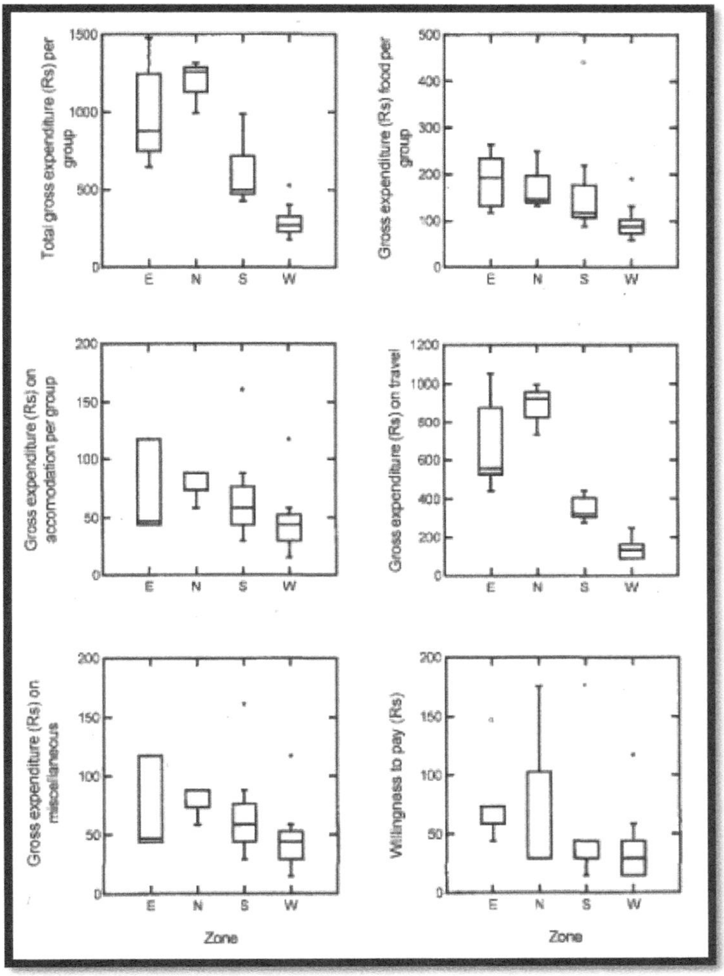

Figure 6.2: Box-Whisker Plot Showing Expenditure and Willingness to Pay for Conservation by Visitors from Four Zonal (E=East, N=North, S=South and W=West) Areas of Sikkim.

The central horizontal lines mark the medians of samples, the edges of the boxes mark the first and third quintiles and the whiskers show the range of the values. Values outside the inner fences are called 'outside values' and plotted with asterisks, and values outside the outer fences, called 'far outside values', are plotted with empty circles. Four zones are east, north, south, and west. The lake is located in the west district.

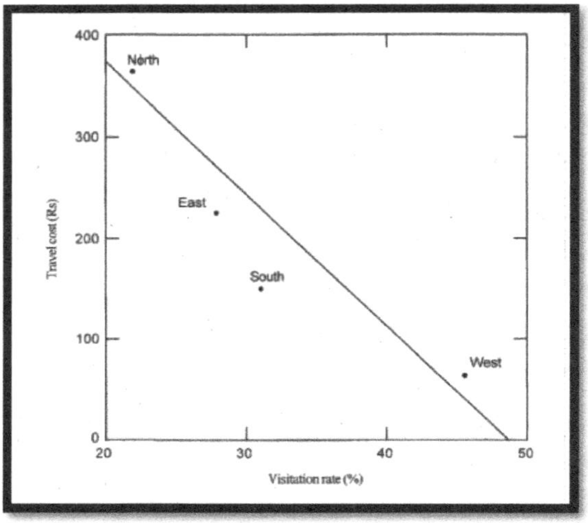

Figure 6.3: Travel Cost and Visitation Rate of Local Pilgrims to the Khecheopalri Lake from the Four Zones (East, North, South, and West). The Lake Is Located in the West District.

Chapter 7 | Tourism, Economic Development and Conservation

7.1. Introduction

Sikkim Himalaya is a site of high biodiversity value, and one that is facing growing threats from a variety of sources, including commercial logging, farming practices, and tourism. As concern grows over the loss of both natural and cultural heritage in this region, attention is turning to strategies which seek to link conservation with tourism development and generate incentives to conserve the resources on which economic benefits depend. Sikkim is growing in popularity and is likely to attract increasing numbers of tourists to visit the area's cultural sites and protected areas of high biodiversity value. The economic significance of the tourism industry is multifarious. Tourism development has a great deal of appeal for its role in the economic development of remote mountain regions and its impact on local society, economy, and the environment. The most important economic benefits of tourism are the earnings of convertible foreign exchange (Malhotra, 1998). However, the criticism of tourism parallels a general paradigm shift away from purely growth-oriented economic development toward more sustainable forms of development (Friedmann et al., 1980; Redclift, 1987; and Brookfield, 1988). The new paradigm requires programs that limit the negative effects of economic behaviour on local environments and cultures. It proposes linkages between economy, culture and ecology in what Norgaard (1984) calls "Co-evolutionary development" and what others have termed "ecodevelopment" (Farvar & Glaeser, 1979). Lee (1988) observes, "There is no other international trading activity which involves such a critical interplay among economic, political, environmental, and social elements as tourism." Brockelman (1988) and McKean (1989) view tourism as a way to foster meaningful cross-cultural relationships as well as to promote environmental conservation and a more equitable distribution of tourism earnings.

This chapter describes tourism in Sikkim, where tourists visit remote natural and cultural settings and discusses its contribution to the state and local economy. This chapter specifically links tourism in mountain regions with sustainable development by examining how tourism connects different stakeholders with broader economic development and contributes to the conservation of valuable biological resources.

7.2. Methods

Participatory Rural Appraisal (PRA) approaches and methods have been used to generate the information. The study has employed a range of PRA tools, including key informant interviews with elderly individuals, group discussions, and transect walks. The techniques have been modified to a great extent, and several innovative approaches have been introduced during the study period at both sites. The participants were involved in a skill development training program from the initial stages of the planning process for conservation management. The secondary data have been generated from government departments.

The study includes visits to various government and private agencies to gather information on national/state tourism policies and travel industry promotions.

7.3. Tourism and Development of Local and Regional Economy

Tourism is a multifaceted economic asset. By itself, it is a "smokeless industry" and is a representation of a cross-section of the whole economy. As such, it is an effective tool of economic growth as far as the tourist places are concerned. A popular tourism attraction is a bonanza for a place. Thus, tourism attractions are distinct and unique economic resources. Therefore, the people of Sikkim have oriented their economy towards tourism. Since 1990, involvement in tourism-related activities has increased in most parts of the State. Most of the tourism earnings come from organized package tours. Some people work exclusively for the Himalayan Mountaineering Institute (HMI) training courses as pack animal porters. However, employment opportunities for women are negligible in trekking and mountaineering courses. A small number of women work in tour operators' offices as receptionists. Employment in trekking and mountaineering is seasonal. Most porters, pack-animal operators and cooks work not more than four to five months a year, but most men are employed on a long-standing basis by a Gangtok-based tour operator. A similar situation is also prevalent in the

Nepalese Himalayas (Adams, 1992). Skilled tour guides and cooks receive salaries year-round, even though they work less than half the year. This employment has a low opportunity cost; other wage-earning employment in Yuksam and around the Khecheopalri Lake is scarce, and it is mainly low-paid day labour.

The Yuksam people began to establish a tourism business in the 1960s, and by 1998, about 69% of all households operated lodges/hotels, shops, and provided porters. These establishments offer visitors snack food, canned goods, and souvenirs. Lodges have become an increasingly important part of the regional economy. An immensely popular investment in tourism since the 1990s is purchasing and keeping packstock for trekking and mountaineering courses.

The multiplier effects of the cash earned in tourism have both increased non-tourism employment and enlarged the market for local agricultural products. The net State Domestic Product (SDP) of Sikkim at constant prices significantly increased from Rs 3316867904 in 1991-92 to Rs 5856043839 (Personal Communication, Bureau of Economics and Statistics, Government of Sikkim).

The sectoral distribution indicates that the tertiary sector predominates, contributing nearly 43% of the total SDP. The annual economic growth rate has been below the national growth rate over the past few years. Thus, tourism is a major sector and should be considered the prime area for promoting sustainable development initiatives.

7.4. Government Investments

The ninth five-year plan of the Sikkim Government had only Rs. 40 million directly allocated to the tourism sector. However, with the advent of the present regime in 1995, a greater focus on tourism had been evident. A specific tourism "Master Plan" for the next five years, commencing that year, with an anticipated budget of over Rs 30 crores, had been developed to promote the tourism industry as a sustainable economic activity. The department prepared a five-circuit project report, in which two were on religious/heritage trails and three were on nature trails. The Government of India allotted Rs. 20 million and the State Government allotted Rs. 12 million for infrastructure development, renovation and refurbishment of monasteries and heritage sites (Anonymous, 1997).

The investment in key infrastructure development by the State Government was Rs 41715000 in 1998-99. The thrust of the State investments is to foster and develop tourism. Out of the total investments, a major portion (50%) is for accommodation and transport services, followed by 12% in advertisements, 5% in event organizations, 1% each in printing and public relations and 30% for other purposes (Anonymous, 1997).

Assistance from the Central Government is often less available than anticipated. One illustrative case is the development of Helicopter services in the State. The State Government expected the Centre to provide almost full assistance.

7.5. Components of Ecotourism and Conservation

The study focuses its work on three key areas that link conservation with ecotourism enterprises. As part of the strategy of biodiversity conservation, increase stakeholder participation in tourism development and natural resource conservation through activities in the investigated areas. The hypothesis is that if income generation is dependent on the continued availability of biodiversity, then those entrepreneurs and stakeholders will have to act upon economic incentives to conserve the resources (protected areas and other natural features) on which income depends.

7.5.1. Participatory Ecoturism Planning

Innovation and empowerment through learning and skill development feature strongly in the Sikkim Biodiversity and Ecotourism project. Participants in community ecotourism plans, training courses and conservation management are all using and developing new participatory learning tools that build upon best practices and positive attributes of Sikkim's natural and cultural heritage. A combination of Appreciative Inquiry and modified Participatory Learning and Action (PLA) tools provides the basis for planning, implementing and evaluating community ecotourism activities (Sharma et al., 2000).

A critical element of planning and subsequent actions in ecotourism is a focus on appreciative inquiry, which involves finding and building upon positive attributes and values within local environments and stakeholder groups. In May 1996, participatory community ecotourism planning was conducted in the Yuksam and the Khecheopalri Lake area by the Sikkim Biodiversity and Ecotourism Project (Plates 3e & 3f). The participants gathered information and generated site-specific ideas for linking tourism-related income-generating activities to conservation efforts, with the aim of encouraging visitors to extend their stay in the village and conserve the natural resources in the area. Local community members felt that the opportunity for increased income generation lay in trying to extend the stay of visitors to the area.

The critical element of planning and subsequent actions in ecotourism is the focus on positive attributes and values of the local environment. All participants were asked to "Discover" the elements in their environment and community that represent the best of what they are and what they do. In addition to the activities identified in May, in October 1996, 28 village members organized their own clean-up campaign of the major trekking route, generating a small initial amount of funds for further activities through recycling bottles and tins. Yuksam and the Khecheopalri residents have readily accepted the principle of local contributions to conservation activities and enthusiastically attended the training courses, as well as showing a keen interest in enterprises such as low-cost covered vegetable production. As a result of the lodge operators' training, participants have developed an agreed tariff and standardized menu. Operators now maintain visitors' registers and issue receipts to customers. Community-wide events, such as income-generating activities through extended visits, including clean-ups and afforestation, were particularly well attended. Between May and December 1996, a series of projects and events catalyzed community members to form the Khangchendzonga Conservation Committee (KCC). KCC has developed a Code of Conduct for visitors and tour operators to follow the ethics of conservation in the area (Table 7.1). Signboards with the code and paid for by KCC have been erected in Yuksam, and visitors now receive a copy of the code at the lodges/hotels. Yuksam community members participated as resource persons for a community ecotourism planning effort at the sacred Khecheopalri Lake site.

The Code of Conduct (COC) was broadly divided into seven points. The compliance of the code of conduct was measured on a five-point scale: "strongly agree ", "agree", "neutral", "disagree", and "strongly disagree". Table 7.1 reveals the details of the indexing and response rate of the tour operators complying with the COC. Among all the issues, it has been observed that 58% of the tour operators strongly agreed to comply properly with the COC.

7.5.2. Participatory Conservation Practices

Despite all the claims of good governance and sustainable management, it is clear that the tremendous growth of nature-based tourism has not been matched by official efforts to adequately plan, implement and monitor developments through an administrative and legal mechanism. A community-based conservation approach to achieve sustainable tourism is being tested in the study sites. This program can foster changes in local attitudes towards conservation and ultimately have the intended result. A critical element developed by community participants during participatory planning was conservation-related activities, including a clean-up campaign, site beautification, and tree plantation in and around their village. In the first phase, a local clean-up of the village was conducted by school teachers, children, and community members (Plate 4b). During the second phase, villagers proposed raising funds for garbage management and an environmental awareness drive for both visitors and community members. The positive reaction among the village community members was evident as shopkeepers and Sunday market hawkers collected their trash and burned it all. The shops were advised to minimize the use of plastic bags, mineral water bottles and to keep trash bins for the collection of garbage. In addition to the activities identified by the local community members, the Khangchendzonga Conservation Committee organized their own clean-up campaign of the major trekking route, generating an initial fund for further activities through the sale of bottles and tins collected during the clean-up campaign (Table 7.2).

To beautify the surrounding locality, indigenous fruit and flower-bearing species were sorted out and planted with the active participation of schoolchildren and the village community. The choice of the species was participatory. At Tshoka, along the trekking trail, the village community contributed significantly to constructing a toilet, mainly for the porters and trekking support staff. The evaluation of these activities, which were conducted annually, reflected the pride taken by the local people and ensured their continuity.

7.5.3. Skill Development Training Program

Ecotourism programs are based on tourism management plans developed in consultation with the local people. The community identifies different training programs, which are designed at the project sites with input from various stakeholder groups. Some of the major training imparted by the project to local people and operators includes naturalist guide training, lodge operation, trek cooks and porters, and ecotourism product marketing exclusively for operators (Table 7.3 & Plates 4c & 4d).

The porters' training highlights the responsible role played by the porters in trekking and mountaineering, and how they can significantly contribute to conservation by observing and practising. The impact of the porters' training is quite significant as porters adopt responsible practices and earn recognition by the government, tourists and different stakeholders. In a particular incident, a porter-cum-guide refused to collect fuelwood for a group of trekkers up in the mountains. He was a trained individual, and hence his conservation efforts were later appreciated and highlighted in national papers.

Trek cooks' training emphasizes menu planning, incorporating indigenous food into the trekking menu, using alternative fuels, safety, hygiene, and sanitation. Lodge operators are trained in housekeeping, managing the accounts, menu planning, use of alternative fuel for heating and cooking purposes, hygiene and sanitation and preparation of local cuisine. To boost the local economy of farmers, polyhouse technology, bio-composting, and training in vegetable seed production are imparted.

7.5.4. Study Tours and Exchanges

Study tours and exchanges have been an effective means of learning about the positive and negative impacts of tourism and protected area management. The Sikkim Biodiversity and Ecotourism project organizes various tours, both within and outside Sikkim, for different levels of stakeholders. The farmers' exposure trip to St. Alphonsus at Kurseyang boosted the enthusiasm and knowledge of the farmers, who later successfully adopted some of the techniques.

To understand the various impacts of tourism on mountain environments, to learn about the cultural and traditional practices of a similar site in Nepal, a mixed group of community participants from Sikkim was taken to Langtang, Nepal. The trip was successful, as the participants learned how the people of Langtang had devised mechanisms for conserving their natural and cultural resources. A policy-level study tour was also organized in early 1998 to the Buxa Tiger Reserve and Royal Chitwan National Park in Nepal, where the group comprised government officials from the Planning and Tourism Departments, representatives from the private sector, and community members. This was an opportunity to learn about conservation and tourism-related issues in and around the protected areas. The visit offered an excellent opportunity for participants to engage in discussions about community forest management for ecotourism purposes and to address the natural resource needs of the local population.

As part of the hypothesis to increase income from responsible ecotourism, the trade association of Sikkim and the Travel Agent Association of Sikkim (TAAS) were encouraged to build links with an equivalent association in Nepal, the Trekking Agent Association of Nepal (TAAN) (Plate 4e). Two reciprocal visits were organized for TAAN and TAAS, where workshops on mountain tourism management were held on both occasions.

7.5.5. Tourism Policy

The sectoral approach of different departments was inadequate in addressing the management aspects in a holistic manner. The various private sector stakeholders involved in tourism operations had their own challenges and expected incentives from the government. The local community, an integral component of ecotourism development, had a limited approach to the government, but this was significantly strengthened during the implementation of the Sikkim Biodiversity and Ecotourism project. In due course of time, the local community-based conservation group KCC has been empowered by various agencies to monitor and implement conservation activities. Workshops and meetings organized by the Sikkim Biodiversity and Ecotourism project have increased the level of interaction between the public and private sectors, and awareness of tourism and conservation-related issues. The State Government has incorporated some of the policy issues into the master plan, and establishing the Tourism Development Corporation has moved a step towards privatization for sustainable development.

Conservation requires a range of interventions, and while the enterprise approach will be a key component of future programs in Sikkim, it will not necessarily be the only one. For entrepreneurs to undertake and continue conservation actions that support their livelihoods, it seems critical that they have some level of decision-making power over the resources in question. It appears that unless this is possible, economic benefits from an enterprise are unlikely to be effective as incentives to conserve. In Sikkim, there was little decision-making power over natural resources among the range of entrepreneurs; thus, there would seem to be little chance of economic incentives turning into actions to conserve biodiversity on which tourism depends. In Sikkim, the natural resources have, for the most part, been managed by the State Government, with permits and rights for subsistence extraction given by State departments. Little exists in the way of community management of forests. However, by engaging stakeholders in a debate over the value of biodiversity in the State economy and the most efficient way it can be conserved, local stakeholders at the study sites are now participating in the ongoing discussions over how biodiversity conservation can be conducted. Traditional decision-makers, such as governments, are now increasingly highlighting the important role that local institutions can play. In Sikkim, the most essential features of the enterprise-based approach are to provide a framework for analyzing and developing the potential of tourism for multiple types of stakeholders.

Furthermore, it provides a means to argue that long-term benefits from tourism will be possible only if those whose income depends on the activity have greater decision-making power in natural resource management. As the number of visitors, both domestic and foreign, increases, the need to be proactive in promoting and supporting a responsible tourism ethic among consumers, suppliers and producers alike is imperative. A number of activities have been identified and presented in table 7.4. The players in sustainable development and management, including tourists, tour operators, government authorities, and the general public, are, therefore, called on to find new forms of coexistence and the right solutions for themselves to ensure the survival of the industry. Sikkim has a great potential to increase its revenue through planned tourism if it adopts policies suitable for tourism development.

7.6. Suggestions for Future Management of Tourism

After making an inventory of various tourist attractions, their important features, historical, religious, social, cultural and scenic aspects, and discussing various other significant considerations of tourism and its related phenomena, their existing and potential resources, problems and prospects can be analyzed for the overall planned development of tourism and also for the betterment and maintenance of the sites and heritage. It is essential to conduct an overall evaluation of the tourist resources in light of their market potential.

A number of potential suggestive measures for the management of tourism in mountain areas are as follows:

Consider applying for the entire study area to be scheduled as a World Heritage Site and implement the site management strategies that this would necessitate. Such a designation would protect the sites, act as a stimulus for high-quality tourism, have considerable publicity value and result in increased tourism revenue.

Complete a detailed survey of religious sites in the region with an architectural survey. No records currently exist of the contents of most of the major Gonzpas in the study sites. Funding should be sought for stabilization and restoration of important Gompas frescoes, which are often in poor condition and have suffered from ad hoc treatments. There is a major tourism resource of the area, and as such, should benefit as soon as possible from part of the tourism revenues, or else they may not survive.

Consider limiting visitor numbers, raising the royalty and implementing a ban on camping-based tourism, combined with investment in upgrading existing traditional inns to provide unique visitor accommodation. During peak season, a paying guest system may be introduced. This can be done with the co-operation of the local communities, which will enhance their income.

The higher per capita consumer surplus value and willingness-to-pay by the foreign tourists indicate that an increase in the existing entrance fee for foreign tourists is not likely to affect their visitation rates. Rather, this can generate a considerable income for the park and Lake Authorities. The foreigners are willing to pay a higher entrance fee and other charges. This will be evident from the income and expenditure statements of hotels/lodges at Yuksam. Hotels/lodges are highly profitable, and their demand is ever-increasing.

The existing entrance fee for foreign tourists may be enhanced.

Improve the existing facilities of the interpretation centre at Yuksam in association with any proposed museum development. Such a centre can brief visitors on the unique social and cultural heritage of the region, especially if displays include ethnographic material and if a trained person is available to discuss and interpret material for visitors. High-quality tourism at both sites can be self-sustaining with minimal environmental and cultural damage if a sensible management plan is implemented. However, continued enforcement of the present policy will result in the destruction of the unique character of the area, with the consequence that visitor numbers (and revenue) will fall. Wisely managed tourism in both sites can provide sustained economic benefits.

Revenue generated from tourism in protected areas should be channelled into the protection and management of the resources.

Limiting visitor numbers has been exceptionally successful in Bhutan and can be equally so in Sikkim as well as in the study sites, but government policy must be clearly established and consistent to project an image of a well-managed "quality" industry. Ill-advised pressure from trekking agents in Sikkim should be avoided.

It would be possible to smooth out the seasonality of visits to Sikkim by increasing trekking royalties during the popular (March to May and October to November) period or extending the "shoulder period" by organizing special attractions in the off-season, for example, organizing promotional fairs, cultural shows, music festivals, tea festivals, etc. Offering fabulous discounts on accommodation and meals, a rebate on shopping prices is another way of attracting tourists in the off-season. Moreover, collective advertisements with press releases to Embassies and the travel trade, showcasing all these benefits to tourists, will prove much more fruitful. Another method of attracting tourists during the off-season is to arrange and offer special rates for conventions, conferences, seminars, games, and tournaments at various educational institutions. It is widely proven that local people should be enabled to play a major role in protected area management and that the appropriate partners for protected area tourism would indeed usually be local communities. This may also offer some compensation for local people, especially if they have been displaced or if their access to resources has been reduced or curtailed. In such circumstances, compensation may take the form of capital assistance to develop the tourism venture.

There is a delicate relationship between the lake ecosystem and community beliefs. Religious and cultural practices hold high value in local communities. Traditional and cultural practices must be linked when developing a management and restoration plan. Ecotourism favours the concept of cultural, biological and nature conservation, and also stresses the economic benefits going down to the local community. Therefore, the Khecheopalri Lake, being an important tourism and pilgrimage destination, should be developed in a participatory way by implementing activities related to ecotourism.

Monitoring is a key tool, but one that is poorly or infrequently used. Monitoring the quality of experience of visitors or the use made of protected areas by local communities should be included in the following order: identification; analysis for a particular site; placement of this in a regional context; and monitoring over time.

Code of Conduct	Strongly agreed	Agreed	Neutral	Disagreed	Strongly disagreed
Conserve Sikkim's natural and cultural heritage					
Do not trample high altitude vegetation, do not pick any flowers or medicinal plants	27	33	15	15	10
Do not disturb wildlife or its habitats	21	30	15	24	10
Do not allow clients to purchase endangered animal parts or antique cultural artifacts	58	21	18	3	-
Support local conservation efforts and income generation activities	43	18	27	12	-
Avoid use of fuelwood; use alternative fuels					
Use kerosene, L.P.G. (or other non-wood fuel) for all purpose by all the group members	12	27	27	31	3
Discourage campfires, encourage camp fun	-	13	10	46	3
Follow safely rules when carrying, storing and using kerosene and gas	7	21	30	39	3
Leave all camps and trails clean					
Dispose of litter and all non-biodegradable materials	3	10	6	42	39
Use toilet tents on all treks in an environmentally friendly manner	10	21	6	45	18
Use established campsites and avoid trenching around tents	6	18	3	24	49
Practice Conservation					
Avoid fuel-consumptive menu items, e.g. backed foods and large menu selections	10	15	30	24	21
Re-package food into réusable plastic containers to reduce wastes	6	18	9	24	43
Reduce waste by disposing and repackaging also	-	12	42	46	-
Practice proper hygiene and sanitation					
Teach all staff about personal hygiene, sanitary, kitchen and camp routines	3	33	15	34	15
Properly treat the drinking water and uncooked vegetables for clients	12	45	33	10	-
Dispose of washing and bathing water well away from streams, use biodegradable soaps	4	33	15	33	15
Take responsibility for staff and porter welfare					
Provide adequate warm clothing and other essentialities	3	18	10	69	-
Periodically train staff in first aid, guide responsibilities and sanitation etc.	6	24	7	45	18
Properly brief clients before leaving on a trek					
Address cultural do's and don'ts	3	18	9	70	-
Plan days for proper altitude acclimatization	7	24	6	45	18

Table 7.1. Perception of Tour Operators on Compliance of Code of Conduct (%) (Strongly Agreed, Neutral, Disagreed)

Activities	Yuksam-Dzongri-Goechha La trekking Corridor			Khecheopalri Lake		
	Male	Female	Total	Male	Female	Total
Clean-up campaign	61	44	105	15	11	26
Tree plantation	104	43	147	10	7	17
Trail maintenance	28	11	39	-	-	-
Lake clean-up	7	3	10	7	6	13
Renovation of monastery	-	-	-	21	4	25
Total	208	101	309	53	28	81

Table 7.2: Participation of Local Communities in Conservation Related Activities in the Study Sites

Training Type	Duration (day)	Participants		
		Male	Female	Total
Porters	2	120	4	124
Cooks	8	31	4	35
Trek cooks	4	20	-	20
Lodge operators	7	26	14	40
Green vegetable production	4	7	2	9
Seed production and vegetable growing	4	13	10	23
Naturalist guide	6	17	2	19
TAAS guide	4	11	2	13
TAAS marketing course	2	13	3	16
Institutional strengthening	2	6	4	10

Table 7.3: Skill Development Training Program Organized in the Study Sites and Number of Participants

Components of responsible tourism	Travel Agencies and Tour Operator	Government Authorities	Lodge/Hotels and Restaurants	Local Community	Tourists
Information for the tourists	Encourage code of conduct that respects the wildlife and culture in the destination	Provide information about the area's natural and cultural values	Provide information on public transport and complementary activities	Organize activities that provide a chance to get to know local values	Find out about local values and problems
Safeguard Destination	Guides are well acquainted with natural values and local environmental problems	Area planning follows environmental criteria and respects the architectural heritage	Carry out environmental impact studies; put restoration before new construction	Plan activities so that they do not have a negative impact	Choose offers that do not hav an environmental impact; do not expect star facilities
Maintain Biodiversity	Destinations whose biodiversity is threatened or vulnerable are not offered	Protect and signpost valuable on vulnerable areas	Buildings and grounds are planned to blend with landscape	Always avoid risking disturbance or damage	Respect animals and plants; do not buy them as souvenirs
Culture	Guides have a good knowledge of the culture and religion of the host place	Maintain cultural identity; plan tourism so that it benefits all local residents	Provide comfort in keeping with local living standards; offer traditional food	Help integrate tourists in the local way of life	Meet the local population; buy traditional arts and crafts
Save Energy	The visits on offer are nearby and/or accessible by public transport and encourage alternative for fuel wood	Facilitate public transport rather than motor cars; protect pedestrian areas	Adopt energy saving measures and encourage clients to collaborate	Avoid activities that consume fossil fuels	Use public transport, trek; discharge campfires, encourage alternatives to fuel wood
Save Water	Destinations with problems of water shortage or purification are not offered	Install treatment plants and promote economy measures	Install economy mechanisms and encourage clients to collaborate	Avoid activities that squander water or that have an impact on water resources	Save water and avoid wasteful activities
Solid waste	Advertising leaflets; use recycled paper; provide solid waste disposals	Organize selective collection and recycling; carry out awareness campaigns	Reduce the use of non-recyclable materials	Use equipment and materials that do not generate waste	Avoid non-recyclable containers; always use litter baskets

Table 7.4: Components and Responsibility for Sustainable Tourism. Components of Travel Agencies and Tour Government Authorities, Lodges/Hotels and Local Community Tourists, Responsible Operator, Restaurants, Tourism

Summary

The magnificent, diverse landscapes and rich cultural heritage of Sikkim have contributed to the rapid growth of tourism. The Sikkim Himalaya has become the foremost centre of trekking and mountaineering in the Hindu-Kush Himalayan region. Its unique flora and fauna, rugged terrain and religio-cultural history make it a place of environmental pilgrimage. Trekking tourism links this once relatively remote part of the world with the global economy and provides new opportunities for economic development. There has been a considerable economic benefit to the local population, which was previously largely dependent on subsistence farming or the government sector for employment. The changes are most strikingly evident in the Yuksam and the Khecheopalri Lake area, where the economic development of the different stakeholders contrasts sharply with the living standards of nearby people who have not become involved in the tourism sector. It is too early to proclaim that this region is a model for achieving local development through tourism. However, the experience to date suggests that locally based tourism development is possible in formerly remote areas, offering hope that the environmental and socio-cultural effects of tourism can be addressed through the combined efforts of local residents, community institutions, national and state policies and institutions, concerned operators of tourism businesses, and responsible tourists.

The present study on "Economic Benefits and Conservation Linkages from Tourism Development in the Sikkim Himlaya" was undertaken with the following main objectives:

- To study and compare the relationships between tourism, market trends, tourism-related revenue distribution patterns, and to predict the impact of future growth in two sites (Yuksam and Khecheopalri) of West Sikkim;
- To assess and identify possible interventions that strengthen the capability of local people and local communities to derive maximum economic benefits from tourism and
- To identify mechanisms for increasing entrepreneurial skills and capacities to expand resources among local stakeholders involved in

ecologically sound and socially responsible tourism and other development activities.

The Yuksam-Dzongri-Goechha La trekking corridor, with an altitudinal variation of 1750-3700 m above sea level, is a 45 km long trek located in the southwestern part of Khangchendzonga National Park. On this corridor, Yuksam is the only settled village, with 11 settlements and 274 households with a total population of 1572. Another site, the sacred Khecheopalri Lake, is situated in the midst of a forest, revealing its pristine setting at an altitude of 1,700 m above sea level in the western part of Sikkim. The lake has a watershed area of 12 km2, of which 91 ha drains directly to the lake and bog.

Salient Findings

1. The number of tourists visiting Sikkim has been growing at a very fast rate in recent years. The main reason for this high growth in tourist influx is the relaxation of regulations, which has opened up a number of new areas for both domestic and foreign visitors. Additionally, tourist facilities have developed in Sikkim as a whole in recent years. The real growth in tourist numbers in Sikkim began in 1980. Until 1980, the state hosted only 10,000 visitors, which eventually increased to more than ten times in 1998. In 1989, about 46416 visitors arrived in Sikkim, of which 96% were domestic and 4% were foreign visitors, while in 1998, about 143410 tourists visited Sikkim, of which 93% were domestic and 7% were foreign visitors.
2. Tourism in the study sites is a highly seasonal activity. The flow of visitors distinctly has two peaks annually, with a low profile from January to March and from July to September, and a high inflow from mid-March to June and from October to mid-December. During the spring and autumn seasons, the Sikkim Himalaya offers ideal conditions for recreation and trekking.
3. The Yuksam-Dzongri-Goechha La corridor inside the Khangchendzonga National Park is the most popular trekking destination in Sikkim. Trekking/adventure travel on this trail started in 1960. Sikkim State opened its borders to foreigners in 1980. The rise of Sikkim's popularity as a nature travel destination began in 1990. The period 1992-97 showed a steady rise in the number of tourists who entered for trekking purposes. In 1997, about 2002

visitors came exclusively to trek in the high mountains. The Himalayan Mountaineering Institute (HMI) also conducted 8 training courses consisting of 1379 trainees.

4. In 1998, out of 143410 visitors coming to Sikkim, only 13% arrived at the Khecheopalri Lake. There is a general perception that the majority of tourists come for recreation, but in the case of the Khecheopalri Lake, visitors come for both recreation and pilgrimage. The data on tourists' flow in this lake are not properly recorded and maintained. The number of visitors has grown from 16068 in 1997 to 18713 in 1998. During 1998, the total number of visitors was 10913 tourists and 7800 pilgrims.
5. As per the purpose or reason for visit to the area, pleasure is the most important reason for visit for all categories of tourists. It has been observed that pilgrimage is the main purpose of visiting the Khecheopalri Lake, while the Yuksam-Dzongri-Goechha La corridor has been used mainly for trekking purposes.
6. The lack of promotional measures in Sikkim is a significant hindrance to selling its tourism products. Currently, the promotional activities undertaken by Sikkim-based tour operators include advertising in Indian newspapers and magazines, as well as direct sales to walk-in clients. A few operators with proven services are also handling referral business from Nepal. Additionally, a few of them are handling business from foreign individual motivators and agents. Some operators have established electronic communication channels, while others maintain a website.
7. About 15 TAAS (Travel Agent Association of Sikkim) agents actively operated treks on the Yuksam-Dzongri-Goechha La route with 303 pax (persons), and non-TAAS members operated treks with 591 pax in 1997. A few agents also operated short treks or walks on the Pemayangtse/Khecheopalri/Yuksam/Tashiding route. The trek price for foreign visitors varied between US$25 and US$50 per person per day, depending on the group size and services provided. Sometimes the trek price has been as low as US$15 per person per day in a competitive situation or for walk-in clients, where the service level is likely to be sacrificed. Agents who are more aware of the trek market in Nepal and other parts of India have quoted between US$35 and US$60 per pax per day to position the product more realistically in terms of competitive trek products

in Nepal. But there are also low-quality treks being operated by some agents who undertake treks for clients at a given price. The trek price is low for domestic visitors, ranging from US$15 to US$35 per person per day, depending on the quality of service. Most of the income generated by the tour operators is from guided treks. The estimated total turnover from tourism was Rs. 117,292,800 (US$286,080) in 1998. Only 13 agents are spending 10 to 25% of revenue on marketing activity.

8. The multiplier effect of revenue earned in tourism has increased non-tourism employment and expanded the market for local agricultural products. The net State Domestic Product of Sikkim (SDP) at constant prices significantly increased from Rs. 3316867904 in 1993-94 to Rs. 5856043839 in 1997-98. The sectoral distribution indicates that the tertiary sector predominates, contributing nearly 43% of the total SDP.
9. The overall literacy rate is significantly higher in the Yuksam area than in the Khecheopalri. The female literacy rate (43% and 46%) is lower than the male literacy rate (54% and 57%) at both sites. Stakeholder-wise, in the Yuksam and Khecheopalri area, the highest literacy rates (74% and 80%) are recorded among families of hotel/lodge owners.
10. In 1996, out of the total 274 households, only 133 households were involved in the tourism sector, which increased to 174 in 1997 and reached 189 by the end of 1998. In Yuksam, 69% of the total households are involved in tourism-related activities. Out of that, 5% are engaged in hotels/lodges, followed by 14% pack-animal operators, 66% porters, 9% fair price shop owners and 6% tea stall owners. At the Khecheopalri Lake site, only 3% of the total population is involved in the tourism sector, as the majority of tourists are day visitors who spend only 2 to 3 hours.
11. In the Yuksam-Dzongri-Goechha La corridor, about 13.07% of the land is owned by the lodge/hotel owners, followed by 11.40% by pack animal operators and 11.68% by the porters. The fair-price shop owners have only 1.65% of the total land, while the rest is owned by non-tourism-involved families. The tea shop owners do not possess any land in Yuksam, as most of them are outsiders who migrated to Yuksam from Bihar. At the Khecheopalri Lake site,

only 11% of the land is owned by households involved in the tourism sector, and 89% is owned by non-tourism-related families.

12. The growth in the number of visitors has led to significant changes in employment and income generation, resulting in improved socioeconomic conditions for the local population. People of both sites have reoriented their local economy around tourism. In 1997, about 46% and 7% of the households had income from this source. Since then, involvement in tourism-related activities has risen to 69% and 22% in 1998.
13. The economic well-being of any region usually refers to the accumulation of various possessions by the family and the source of income. In 1997, the total income of all stakeholders in the Yuksam and Khecheopalri area was Rs. 662,2983 and Rs. 969,800, which increased to Rs. 712,4146 and Rs. 107,5130 in 1998. In 1998, in the Yuksam area, the people involved in the tourism sector contributed 70% of the total income, whereas the non-tourism sector contributed 30%. In Khecheopalri, the tourism sector contributed 30% of the total income, and the non-tourism sector contributed 70%. Economic development leads to a change in food consumption patterns as income increases. With an increase in income, total calorie intake and the consumption of other foods increase.
14. Analysis of forest and other land uses reveals that dense mixed forests have decreased in the past few decades, with an increase in open mixed and degraded forests. The five class-I land uses have been identified as occurring in both sites. A total of 84% and 77% of the lake and trekking corridor area have forests. The majority (34%) of the forestland is under degraded category (crown cover, 20%), 19% are open forest (crown cover 21-40%) and 19% are dense forest (crown cover > 40%) in Yuksam-Dzongri-GoechhaLa corridor, whereas in the Khecheopalri Lake site, it is dominated by open mixed forest (41%), followed by dense mixed forest (23%) and degraded forest (21%). Agriculture is the predominant non-forest land-use, occupying about 14% of the total area in the trekking corridor and 13% at the Lake site. About 3% and 1% area fall under the wasteland category (rock outcrop and landslide). In the case of the lake area, major changes have been recorded in the form of bog area expansion. The conversion of dense mixed forest

to open mixed forest and then to degraded forests has been mainly attributed to fuelwood and timber extraction, fodder collection and grazing. Agricultural land expansion in the lake watershed has a major impact on the lake ecosystem through increased sediment deposition.

15. The high demand for fuelwood, fodder and timber poses a threat to the surrounding area of the Yuksmn-Dzongri-Goechha La corridor and the Khecheopalri Lake area. Chopping and lopping of highly preserved tree species for fuelwood, fodder and timber has put tremendous pressure on some selective species in this area.
16. The fuelwood consumption rate was 24 kg/day, as estimated for households in the area during 1997-98. Consumption of the commercial alternative source of energy, i.e., kerosene and LPG (14% and 3%, respectively), is insignificant. There is no evidence of non-conventional sources of energy being used by any of the stakeholders. The consumption rate of fuelwood varies among different stakeholders. A total of 2437 Mg yr-I of fuelwood is consumed by stakeholders at the Yuksam village, out of which 2264 Mg yr-I is consumed by the local community, followed by 101 Mg yr-I consumed by hotels and lodges, 45 Mg yr-I consumed by HMI, and 26 Mg yr-I consumed by other stakeholders. Whereas in the case of Khecheopalri, a total of 1126 Mg yr-I is consumed, out of which 670 Mg yr-I is consumed by the local community and 456 Mg yr-I is consumed by the trekker's hut and tea shops.
17. Animal husbandry in both sites is mainly dependent on the surrounding forests. These forests are heavily lopped along the trail route, lake-surrounding forests, and the margins of the settlements. The grazing pressure of Yaks and Dzos is seasonal and more prominent in the alpine zone. The livestock populations of the Yuksam-Dzongri-Goechha La corridor increased from 1530 in 1996 to 1708 in 1998, whereas there were 304 domesticated animals in the Khecheopalri lake area. The Yaks/Dzos and cattle need about 33 kg of green fodder per day, whereas sheep and goats require about 15 kg per day.
18. A survey of households in the villages of the Yuksam and the Khecheopalri Lake area has shown that a double-storied building/lodge needs about 600 to 700 ft3 of wood. Generally, large

timber poles are harvested for making ceilings, doors, windows and beams. Medium-sized poles are used for furniture and repairs. Small-sized poles (mainly bamboo) are cut for making cattle sheds or temporary huts.

19. Dependence on fuelwood for energy is causing serious deforestation problems in the trekking corridor and the Lake site. The pressure is far greater in Monastery forest than in the trail forest outside the Khangchendzonga National Park. The consumption of fuelwood varies amongst stakeholders with respect to different physical and economic factors, causing serious deforestation problems in the trail and the Lake site. The widespread switching over to inferior quality of fuelwood species is an indicator of pressure in the forests of both sites. The fuelwood continues to be the prime source for cooking in the trekking corridor, while commercial alternative energy sources contribute very little. Enhancing the supply of fuelwood through plantations and reducing the fuelwood demand through providing an alternative source of energy can facilitate this.
20. The heavy inflow of visitors during the religious festival has shown some negative impacts on the serenity of the lake, especially in the form of noise, littering, garbage dumps, and resource extraction. Garbage quantification in 1998 after the festival showed that the total garbage collected was 452 kg, out of which 62% were biodegradable and 38% were non-biodegradable wastes. The total garbage collected during the tourist season was 2375 kg in and around the lake.
21. The economic valuation of ecotourism has been conducted in the Yuksam-Dzongri-Goechha La corridor and the Khecheopalri Lake area. A contingent valuation method has been used to estimate the Willingness-to-pay (WTP) for conservation and protection of natural resources in both sites. The results show that the response is emphatically positive. The survey has received a positive response from local communities, pilgrims, and both domestic and foreign visitors, demonstrating their willingness to conserve the area. The analysis reports a mean WTP per visitor per visit that is higher for foreign visitors than for domestic visitors. Local community members are also willing to pay for environmental management. The multiple regression on WTP reveals that the attitudes of

respondents, their visitation rate, and the number of aspects of the area they consider valuable are essential determinants of WTP for the trekking corridor and the Lake site. Variables have attained the expected sign, and they are statistically significant.

22. As per the contingent valuation method for the entire sample, using mean of variables, the estimated willingness-to-pay for the management of trekking corridor and the sacred Khecheopalri Lake are US$8.84 and US$7.19 by the foreign visitors and US$ 1.91 and US$2.51 by the domestic visitors per trip, whereas US$6.20 and US$0.88 for local community annually and US$2.16 for local pilgrims per visit, respectively. This indicates that foreign visitors have a higher recreational/conservation value than domestic visitors and local community members.
23. Incorporating the estimated values of the consumer surplus for their visit to the Khecheopalri Lake, which are derived as US$661 and US$1562 in the first and second equations, respectively, as per the travel cost method. Recreational/Sacredness value per visitor is US$3.87 as per the consumer surplus. The total number of local pilgrims to the Khecheopalri Lake was 7800 in 1998, and the annual aggregate recreational/sacredness value for the pilgrims amounted to US$30186.
24. The Lake site has recreational and biodiversity values for domestic and foreign visitors, as well as a greater spiritual significance for the Sikkimese people. The demand curve function for recreation increases with a decrease in travel cost and distance for Sikkimese pilgrims. The Lake site has demonstrated high recreational/sacredness values, which are attributed to the conservation of the site for biodiversity and pilgrims.
25. The hypothesis is that if income generation is dependent on the continued availability of biodiversity, then those entrepreneurs and stakeholders will have to act upon economic incentives to conserve the resources on which income depends. This hypothesis holds true at both sites. Several conservation-related activities have been organized by stakeholders to conserve and clean the area.
26. The issues addressed in this study, regarding conservation involvement, socio-economics, and substitutability, aim to facilitate

a deeper understanding of the role of ecotourism in conservation efforts.

References

1. Ableson, P. (1979). *Cost-benefit analysis and environmental problems.* London, UK: Saxon House.
2. Adams, V. (1992). Tourism and Sherpa, Nepal: Reconstruction of reciprocity. *Annals of Tourism Research, 19*, 534–554.
3. Adventure Travel Society. (1998). *Press release – Adventure Travel Congress.* Colorado, USA.
4. Agarwal, B. (1989). Rural women's poverty and natural resource sustenance, sustainability and struggle for change. *Economic and Political Weekly, 24*, 46–65.
5. Allcock, A., Jones, B., Lane, S., & Grant, J. (1994). *National ecotourism strategies.* Canberra: Commonwealth of Australia.
6. Anonymous. (1997). *Tourism master plan of Sikkim, 1997–2011.* Department of Tourism, Government of Sikkim.
7. Arrow, K. J., Solow, R., Leamer, E., Portney, P., Radner, R., & Schuman, H. (1993). Report of the NOAA panel on contingent valuation. *Federal Register, 58*, 4601–4614.
8. Banskota, K., & Sharma, B. (1995). *Mountain tourism for local community development* (Discussion Paper No. MEI 95/11). Kathmandu, Nepal: International Centre for Integrated Mountain Development (ICIMOD).
9. Banskota, K., & Upadhyay, M. (1991). *Impacts of rural tourism on environment, income, and employment: Implications for tourism development in the Makalu Barun Conservation Area.* Kathmandu, Nepal: Makalu-Barun Conservation Project.
10. Bergstrom, J. C., Stoll, J. R., Titre, J. P., & Wright, V. L. (1990). Economic value of wetlands-based recreation. *Ecological Economics, 2*, 129–147.
11. Bishop, R. C., & Heberlein, T. A. (1992). The contingent valuation method. In K. M. Ward & J. W. Duffield (Eds.), *Natural resource damages: Law and economics* (pp. 281–309). New York, NY: John Wiley and Sons.

12. Bjonness, I. (1980). Animal husbandry and grazing, a conservation and management problem in Sagarmatha (Mt. Everest) National Park (SNP), Nepal. *Norsk Geografisk Tidsskrift, 3*(4), 59–76.
13. Blangy, S., & Wood, M. E. (1992, February 10–21). Developing and implementing ecotourism guidelines for wildlands and neighbouring communities. Paper presented at the IV World Congress on National Parks and Protected Areas, Caracas, Venezuela.
14. Boo, E. (1990). *Ecotourism: The potentials and pitfalls* (Vols. I & II). Washington, DC: WWF.
15. Bouwes, N. W., & Schneider, R. (1979). Procedures in estimating benefits of water quality change. *American Journal of Agricultural Economics, 61*(3), 535–539.
16. Boyd, S. W., Butler, R. W., Haider, W., & Perera, A. (1994). Identifying areas for ecotourism in Northern Ontario: Application of a geographical information system methodology. *Journal of Applied Recreation Research, 19*, 11–66.
17. Brandon, K., & Hawkins, D. E. (1996). *Ecotourism and conservation: A review of key issues* (Environment Department Paper No. 33). Washington, DC: The World Bank.
18. Broadus, J. M., & Gaines, A. G. (1987). Coastal and marine areas management in the Galapagos Islands. *Coastal Management, 15*, 75–88.
19. Brockelman, W. Y. (1988, August 22–25). The role of nature trekking in conservation. Paper presented at the International Symposium on Nature Conservation and Tourism Development, Surat Thani, Thailand.
20. Brockelman, W. Y., & Dearden, P. (1990). The role of nature trekking in conservation: A case study in Thailand. *Environmental Conservation, 17*, 141–148.
21. Brookfield, H. C. (1988). Sustainable development and the environment. *Journal of Development Studies, 25*, 126–135.
22. Brookshire, D., Eubanks, L. S., & Randall, A. (1983). Estimating option prices and existence values for wildlife resources. *Land Economics, 59*, 1–15.
23. Brown, G., Jr., & Henry, W. (1989). *The economic value of elephants* (Discussion Paper 89–12). London, UK: The London Environmental Economics Centre.

24. Butler, J. R. (1992, February 10–21). Ecotourism: Its changing face and evolving philosophy. Paper presented at the IV World Congress on National Parks and Protected Areas, Caracas, Venezuela.

25. Byers, A. C. (1986). An assessment of landscape change in the Khumbu region of Nepal using repeat photography. *Mountain Research and Development, 7*, 77–81.

26. Caulkins, P., Bishop, R., & Bouwes, N. (1986). The travel cost model for lake recreation: A comparison of two methods for incorporating site quality and substitution effects. *American Journal of Agricultural Economics, 68*, 291–297.

27. Ceballos-Lascurain, H. (1993). *Ecotourism in Central America.* Technical Report for WTO/UNDP Project CAM 790/011.

28. Ceballos-Lascurain, H. (1996). *Tourism, ecotourism and protected areas.* Gland, Switzerland: IUCN.

29. Chopra, K., Chauhan, M., Sharma, S., & Sangeeta, N. (1997). *Economic valuation of biodiversity: A case study of Keoladeo National Park, Bharatpur* (Unpublished report, Part II). Delhi: Institute of Economic Growth.

30. Clawson, M., & Knetsch, J. (1966). *Economics of outdoor recreation: Recreation for the future.* Baltimore, MD: Johns Hopkins University Press.

31. Collins, N. M. (1990). The conservation value of tropical rain forest: A global perspective. In A. Gomez-Pompa, T. C. Whitmore, & M. Hadley (Eds.), *Rain forest regeneration and management* (pp. 47–65). Paris: UNESCO & The Parthenon Publishing Group.

32. Costanza, R., d'Arge, R., de Groot, R., Farber, S., Grasso, M., Hannon, B., ... & van den Belt, M. (1997). The value of the world's ecosystem services and natural capital. *Nature, 387*, 253–260.

33. Crocker, T. D., & Tschirhart, J. (1992). Ecosystems, externalities and economies. *Environmental and Resource Economics, 2*, 551–567.

34. Dixon, J. A., & Sherman, P. B. (1990). *Economics of protected areas: A new look at benefits and costs.* Washington, DC: Island Press.

35. Dixit, K. K. (1997). Impact of tourism on environment in the mountain areas. In B. Thapa (Ed.), *Issues in tourism in the mountain regions.* Kathmandu: ICIMOD.

36. Drijver, C. A. (1990). People's participation in environmental projects in developing countries. *Landscape and Urban Planning, 20*(1–3), 129–139.
37. Duffield, J. (1984). Travel cost and contingent valuation: A comparative analysis. *Journal of Environmental Economics and Management, 11*(2), 175–187.
38. Eagles, P. F. J. (1992). The travel motivations of Canadian ecotourists. *Journal of Travel Research, 31*(2), 3–7.
39. Eagles, P. F. J. (1997). International ecotourism management: Using Australia and Africa as case studies. *Paper presented at the IUCN World Commission on Protected Areas Symposium on Protected Areas in the 21st Century*, Albany, Australia.
40. Edwards, S. F. (1991). The demand for non-consumptive uses of wildlife. *Land Economics, 67*(2), 221–231.
41. Edwards, S. F., & Anderson, G. D. (1987). Overlooked biases in contingent valuation surveys: Some considerations. *Land Economics, 63*(2), 168–178.
42. FAO. (1988). *Conservation and development of tropical forest resources.* Rome: Food and Agriculture Organization of the United Nations.
43. FAO. (1990). *Sustainable development and natural resources management.* Rome: Food and Agriculture Organization of the United Nations.
44. Fennell, D. A. (1999). *Ecotourism: An introduction.* London: Routledge.
45. Filion, F. L., Foley, J. P., & Jacquemot, A. J. (1994). The economics of global ecotourism. In E. Cater & G. Lowman (Eds.), *Ecotourism: A sustainable option?* (pp. 235–262). Chichester: John Wiley & Sons.
46. Fisher, A. C., & Raucher, R. S. (1984). Intrinsic values of natural areas: Rationality and rational management. *Natural Resources Journal, 24*, 153–166.
47. Freeman, A. M., III. (1993). *The measurement of environmental and resource values: Theory and methods.* Washington, DC: Resources for the Future.
48. Gilmour, D. A., & Fisher, R. J. (1991). *Villagers, forests and foresters: The philosophy, process and practice of community forestry in Nepal.* Kathmandu: Sahayogi Press.
49. Ginsberg, J. R. (1991). *Conservation of endangered species in captivity: An interdisciplinary approach.* Chicago, IL: University of Chicago Press.
50. Goodwin, H., & Swingland, I. R. (1996). Ecotourism, biodiversity and local development. *Biodiversity and Conservation, 5*, 275–276.

51. Gossling, S. (1999). Ecotourism: A means to safeguard biodiversity and ecosystem functions? *Ecological Economics, 29*, 303–320.

52. Government of India. (1988). *National wildlife action plan.* New Delhi: Ministry of Environment and Forests.

53. Government of India. (1992). *National conservation strategy and policy statement on environment and development.* New Delhi: Ministry of Environment and Forests.

54. Government of India. (1993). *Guidelines for eco-development in protected areas.* New Delhi: Ministry of Environment and Forests.

55. Government of Nepal. (1995). *Nepal environmental policy and action plan.* Kathmandu: Ministry of Population and Environment.

56. Green, R., & Paine, R. (1997). *State of the world's protected areas at the end of the twentieth century.* IUCN World Commission on Protected Areas.

57. Gregersen, H. M., & Contreras, A. (1992). Economic assessment of forestry project impacts. *FAO Forestry Paper No. 106.* Rome: Food and Agriculture Organization.

58. Groom, M. J., & Podolsky, R. D. (1990). Conservation of the tropics: A review of patterns and problems. *Tropical Conservation Biology, 4*, 1–17.

59. Grossman, G. M., & Krueger, A. B. (1995). Economic growth and the environment. *Quarterly Journal of Economics, 110*(2), 353–377.

60. Hanemann, W. M. (1991). Willingness to pay and willingness to accept: How much can they differ? *American Economic Review, 81*(3), 635–647.

61. Hanemann, W. M. (1994). Valuing the environment through contingent valuation. *Journal of Economic Perspectives, 8*(4), 19–43.

62. Harcourt, A. H. (1987). Man and gorillas in Africa. In B. B. Smuts, D. L. Cheney, R. M. Seyfarth, R. W. Wrangham, & T. T. Struhsaker (Eds.), *Primate societies* (pp. 539–545). Chicago, IL: University of Chicago Press.

63. Hardin, G. (1968). The tragedy of the commons. *Science, 162*(3859), 1243–1248.

64. Hawkins, D. E. (1994). Ecotourism: Opportunities for developing countries. In E. Cater & G. Lowman (Eds.), *Ecotourism: A sustainable option?* (pp. 49–60). Chichester: John Wiley & Sons.

65. Healy, R. G. (1994). The "common pool" problem in tourism landscapes. *Annals of Tourism Research, 21*(3), 596–611.
66. Heinen, J. T., & Kattel, B. (1992). Parks, people and conservation: A review of management issues in Nepal's protected areas. *Population and Environment, 14*(1), 49–84.
67. Heinen, J. T., & Shrestha, S. K. (2006). Evolving policies for conservation: An historical profile of the protected area system of Nepal. *Journal of Environmental Planning and Management, 49*(1), 41–58.
68. Henry, C. (1974). Option values in the economics of irreplaceable assets. *Review of Economic Studies, 41*(5), 89–104.
69. Hitchcock, M., King, V., & Parnwell, M. (1993). *Tourism in South-East Asia.* London: Routledge.
70. Hitchcock, M., & King, V. (1997). Back to the future: Heritage tourism and society in the Malay world. In M. Hitchcock, V. King, & M. Parnwell (Eds.), *Tourism in South-East Asia* (pp. 91–103). London: Routledge.
71. Honey, M. (1999). *Ecotourism and sustainable development: Who owns paradise?* Washington, DC: Island Press.
72. IUCN. (1980). *World conservation strategy: Living resource conservation for sustainable development.* Gland, Switzerland: International Union for Conservation of Nature.
73. IUCN. (1991). *Caring for the Earth: A strategy for sustainable living.* Gland, Switzerland: IUCN/UNEP/WWF.
74. IUCN. (1994). *Guidelines for protected area management categories.* Gland, Switzerland: IUCN.
75. IUCN. (1996). *1996 IUCN Red List of threatened animals.* Gland, Switzerland: IUCN.
76. James, D., & Burgess, J. (2000). The economics of biodiversity. *Biodiversity Economics, 2*(1), 15–34.
77. Jarvis, L. S. (1980). Cattle as capital goods and ranchers as portfolio managers: An application to the Argentine cattle sector. *Journal of Political Economy, 88*(3), 367–389.
78. Jefferies, M. (1982). The recreational value of Lake District National Park. *Regional Studies, 16*(2), 139–148.
79. Job, H. (1996). Community participation in sustainable tourism development: Approaches to the planning process in the Third World. *International Journal of Environment and Sustainable Development, 5*(3), 173–185.

80. Kahn, J. R. (1995). *The economic approach to environmental and natural resources.* Fort Worth, TX: Dryden Press.

81. Kant, S., & Nautiyal, J. C. (1995). The valuation of environmental services: A case study of the Yamuna River, India. *Journal of Environmental Management, 45*(1), 7–16.

82. Kayastha, S. L. (1992). Tourism and environment: A case study of Nepal. *Geographical Review of India, 54*(1), 36–47.

83. Keliang, Z., & Keeley, J. (2003). Land rights in China: Facts, fiction, and issues. *China Perspectives, 45*(1), 61–74.

84. Khan, M. (1997). Tourism development and dependency theory: Mass tourism vs. ecotourism. *Annals of Tourism Research, 24*(4), 988–991.

85. Kremen, C., Merenlender, A. M., & Murphy, D. D. (1994). Ecological monitoring: A vital need for integrated conservation and development programs in the tropics. *Conservation Biology, 8*(2), 388–397.

86. Krutilla, J. V. (1967). Conservation reconsidered. *American Economic Review, 57*(4), 777–786.

87. Krutilla, J. V., & Fisher, A. C. (1985). *The economics of natural environments: Studies in the valuation of commodity and amenity resources.* Baltimore, MD: Johns Hopkins University Press.

88. Kumari, K. (1995). An environmental and economic assessment of forest management options: A case study in Malaysia. *Environment Department Paper No. 26.* Washington, DC: World Bank.

89. Kunwar, R. R. (1997). *Tourism and development: Science and industry interface.* Kathmandu: Laxmi Kunwar.

90. Laarman, J. G., & Durst, P. B. (1987). Nature travel in the tropics. *Journal of Forestry, 85*(5), 43–46.

91. Laarman, J. G., & Gregersen, H. M. (1996). Pricing policy in nature-based tourism. *Tourism Management, 17*(4), 247–254.

92. Lélé, S. M. (1991). Sustainable development: A critical review. *World Development, 19*(6), 607–621.

93. Lindberg, K. (1991). *Policies for maximizing nature tourism's ecological and economic benefits.* Washington, DC: World Resources Institute.

94. Lindberg, K. (1993). Economic aspects of ecotourism. In K. Lindberg & D. E. Hawkins (Eds.), *Ecotourism: A guide for planners and*

managers (pp. 87–117). North Bennington, VT: The Ecotourism Society.

95. Lindberg, K., Enriquez, J., & Sproule, K. (1996). Ecotourism questioned: Case studies from Belize. *Annals of Tourism Research, 23*(3), 543–562.
96. Lindberg, K., & Hawkins, D. E. (Eds.). (1993). *Ecotourism: A guide for planners and managers.* North Bennington, VT: The Ecotourism Society.
97. Lindberg, K., & Huber, R. (1993). Economic issues in ecotourism management. In K. Lindberg & D. E. Hawkins (Eds.), *Ecotourism: A guide for planners and managers* (pp. 118–136). North Bennington, VT: The Ecotourism Society.
98. Loomis, J. B. (1987). Balancing public trust resources of Mono Lake and Los Angeles' water right: An economic approach. *Water Resources Research, 23*(8), 1449–1456.
99. Loomis, J. B. (1989). Test–retest reliability of the contingent valuation method: A comparison of general population and visitor responses. *American Journal of Agricultural Economics, 71*(1), 76–84.
100. Loomis, J. B. (1992). The evolution of a more rigorous approach to benefit transfer: Benefit function transfer. *Water Resources Research, 28*(3), 701–705.
101. Loomis, J. B., & Walsh, R. G. (1997). *Recreation economic decisions: Comparing benefits and costs* (2nd ed.). State College, PA: Venture Publishing.
102. Loon, R., & Polakow, D. (2001). Ecotourism ventures: Rags or riches? *Annals of Tourism Research, 28*(4), 892–907.
103. Lovelock, J. (1979). *Gaia: A new look at life on earth.* Oxford: Oxford University Press.
104. Maharana, I. (1998). *Economic valuation of ecotourism: A case study of Keoladeo National Park (Bharatpur), Rajasthan* (Unpublished doctoral dissertation). Jawaharlal Nehru University, New Delhi.
105. Maharana, I., Rai, S. C., & Sharma, E. (2000). Valuing ecotourism in a sacred lake of the Sikkim Himalaya, India. *Environmental Conservation, 27*(3), 269–277.
106. McNeely, J. A. (1988). Economics and biological diversity: Developing and using economic incentives to conserve biological resources. *IUCN Publication Services.* Gland, Switzerland.

107. McNeely, J. A. (1993). Parks for life: Report of the 4th World Congress on National Parks and Protected Areas. Gland, Switzerland: IUCN.

108. McNeely, J. A., Thorsell, J., & Ceballos-Lascurain, H. (1992). Guidelines: Development of national parks and protected areas for tourism. Madrid: WTO.

109. Mishra, H. R. (1982). The role of buffer zones and local people in the protected area management. *Tiger Paper, 9*(3), 2–6.

110. Mitchell, R. C., & Carson, R. T. (1989). *Using surveys to value public goods: The contingent valuation method.* Washington, DC: Resources for the Future.

111. Moktan, M. R. (1997). Tourism and environmental implications in the Sikkim Himalaya. *Himalayan Paryavaran, 4*(2), 1–12.

112. Montgomery, C. A., Brown, G. M., & Adams, D. M. (1994). The marginal cost of species preservation: The northern spotted owl. *Journal of Environmental Economics and Management, 26*(2), 111–128.

113. Munasinghe, M. (1993). Environmental economics and biodiversity management in developing countries. *Ambio, 22*(2–3), 126–135.

114. Munasinghe, M., & Lutz, E. (1993). Environmental–economic evaluation of projects and policies for sustainable development. *Environment Working Paper No. 42.* Washington, DC: World Bank.

115. Myers, N. (1996). Environmental services of biodiversity. *Proceedings of the National Academy of Sciences, 93*(7), 2764–2769.

116. Navrud, S., & Mungatana, E. D. (1994). Environmental valuation in developing countries: The recreational value of wildlife viewing. *Ecological Economics, 11*(2), 135–151.

117. Nepal, S. K. (2000). Tourism in protected areas: The Nepalese Himalayan experience. *Tourism Recreation Research, 25*(1), 69–77.

118. Nepal, S. K., & Weber, K. E. (1993). Struggle for existence: Park–people conflict in the Royal Chitwan National Park, Nepal. *Asian Institute of Technology Journal, 14*(1), 67–74.

119. Nepal, S. K., & Weber, K. E. (1995). Prospects for coexistence: Wildlife and local people. *Ambio, 24*(4), 238–245.

120. Nepal, S. K., & Weber, K. E. (1996). Prospects for coexistence: Wildlife and local people in Nepal. *Ambio, 25*(4), 238–245.

121. Norton-Griffiths, M., & Southey, C. (1995). The opportunity costs of biodiversity conservation in Kenya. *Ecological Economics, 12*(2), 125–139.

122. Odeh, I. (1997). *Tourism and the environment: A case study from Palestine.* Jerusalem: Palestinian Academic Society.

123. OECD. (1995). *The economic appraisal of environmental projects and policies: A practical guide.* Paris: Organisation for Economic Co-operation and Development.

124. Orams, M. B. (1995). Towards a more desirable form of ecotourism. *Tourism Management, 16*(1), 3–8.

125. Panayotou, T. (1993). Green markets: The economics of sustainable development. *Environment, 35*(5), 4–10.

126. Panayotou, T. (1994). *Conservation of biodiversity and economic development: The concept of transferable development rights.* Gland, Switzerland: IUCN.

127. Pandey, R. S. (1995). Tourism and environment in the Himalayan region. *Journal of Himalayan Studies, 6*(2), 45–52.

128. Pearce, D. W. (1993). Economic values and the natural world. *Cambridge: MIT Press.*

129. Pearce, D. W., & Moran, D. (1994). The economic value of biodiversity. *London: Earthscan Publications.*

130. Pearce, D. W., & Turner, R. K. (1990). Economics of natural resources and the environment. *Baltimore, MD: Johns Hopkins University Press.*

131. Peters, C. M., Gentry, A. H., & Mendelsohn, R. O. (1989). Valuation of an Amazonian rainforest. *Nature, 339*(6227), 655–656.

132. Peters, J., & Thapa, J. (1994). Sustainable development, biodiversity and livelihood: Issues for Nepal. *ICIMOD Discussion Paper No. MEI 94/3.* Kathmandu, Nepal.

133. Pillai, V. K. (1992). Ecotourism in Kerala: Potentials and constraints. *Kerala Economic Review, 25*(2), 101–107.

134. Piper, S., & Mendelsohn, R. (1991). Valuing the environmental benefits of flood protection using contingent valuation. *Journal of Environmental Economics and Management, 20*(3), 213–225.

135. Poe, G. L., Boyle, K. J., & Bergstrom, J. C. (1994). The reliability of benefit estimates derived from contingent valuation: Evidence from a meta-analysis. *Land Economics, 70*(1), 52–65.

136. Pope, C. A., III. (1985). Agricultural productive and consumptive use components of outdoor recreation benefits. *American Journal of Agricultural Economics, 67*(4), 819–825.
137. Postel, S., Daily, G. C., & Ehrlich, P. R. (1996). Human appropriation of renewable fresh water. *Science, 271*(5250), 785–788.
138. Randall, A. (1991). Total economic value as a basis for policy. *Transactions of the American Fisheries Society, 120*(3), 325–331.
139. Randall, A., & Stoll, J. R. (1983). Existence value in a total valuation framework. In R. D. Rowe & L. G. Chestnut (Eds.), *Managing air quality and scenic resources at national parks and wilderness areas* (pp. 265–274). Boulder, CO: Westview Press.
140. Rausser, G. C., & Small, A. A. (2000). Valuing research leads: Bioprospecting and the conservation of genetic resources. *Journal of Political Economy, 108*(1), 173–206.
141. Repetto, R. (1989). *Economic incentives for sustainable production.* Washington, DC: World Resources Institute.
142. Repetto, R., & Gillis, M. (Eds.). (1988). Public policies and the misuse of forest resources. *Cambridge: Cambridge University Press.*
143. Roe, D., Leader-Williams, N., & Dalal-Clayton, B. (1997). Take only photographs, leave only footprints: The environmental impacts of wildlife tourism. *IIED Wildlife and Development Series No. 10.* London: IIED.
144. Ruitenbeek, J. (1989). Social cost-benefit analysis of the Korup Project, Cameroon. *Report prepared for WWF.* London.
145. Ruitenbeek, J. (1992). Mangrove management: An economic analysis of management options with a focus on Bintuni Bay, Irian Jaya. *Environmental Management, 16*(5), 507–518.
146. Ruitenbeek, J. (1994). Modelling economy–ecology linkages in mangroves: Economic evidence for promoting conservation in Bintuni Bay, Indonesia. *Ecological Economics, 10*(3), 233–247.
147. Sathiendrakumar, R., & Tisdell, C. (1989). Valuation of wildlife recreation: An economic analysis of its importance in the tourism sector of Sri Lanka. *Tourism Recreation Research, 14*(1), 3–12.
148. Shackley, M. (1994). The land of Lo. In A. V. Seaton (Ed.), *Tourism: The state of the art* (pp. 219–228). Chichester: John Wiley & Sons.
149. Shackley, M. (1996). *Wildlife tourism.* London: International Thomson Business Press.

150. Sharma, U. R. (1990). An overview of park–people interactions in Royal Chitwan National Park, Nepal. *Landscape and Urban Planning, 19*(2), 133–144.

151. Sharma, U. R. (1991). Park–people interactions in Royal Chitwan National Park, Nepal. *Ph.D. dissertation, State University of New York, College of Environmental Science and Forestry, Syracuse.*

152. Sharma, U. R., & Shaw, W. W. (1996). Nepal's Royal Chitwan National Park and surrounding population: A sociocultural study. *Environmental Conservation, 23*(3), 235–244.

153. Sharma, U. R., & Shaw, W. W. (1996). Role of tourists in biodiversity conservation in Nepal. *Ambio, 25*(4), 274–281.

154. Sharma, U. R., & Shaw, W. W. (1998). Integrated conservation and development project life cycles in Royal Chitwan National Park, Nepal. *Environmental Conservation, 25*(4), 241–250.

155. Smith, V. K. (1993). Nonmarket valuation of environmental resources: An interpretive appraisal. *Land Economics, 69*(1), 1–26.

156. Smith, V. K., & Desvousges, W. H. (1986). Measuring water quality benefits. *Boston, MA: Kluwer-Nijhoff.*

157. Tisdell, C. (1991). *Economics of environmental conservation: Economics for environmental and ecological management.* Amsterdam: Elsevier.

158. Tisdell, C. (1996). Ecotourism, economics, and the environment: Observations from China. *Journal of Travel Research, 34*(4), 11–19.

159. Tisdell, C., & Broadus, J. M. (1989). Policy issues related to the establishment and management of marine protected areas. *Coastal Management, 17*(1), 37–53.

160. Tisdell, C., & Wen, J. (1991). Investment in ecotourism: Assessing the potential for economic benefits. *Tourism Economics, 5*(1), 5–20.

Photo Plates

Plate 1

(a) View of snowclad mountains from Dzongri is one of the major attraction for the tourists

(b) Tshoka, the last settlement along trekking corridor at 3000 m

(c) Khecheopalri - a sacred lake

(d) Stream trumbling to meet sacred Rathong Chu

(e) Norbugang - 1st Chogyal enthroned in 1642

(f) Dubdi monastery near yuksam

Plate 2

(a) Trekking trail condition at higher elevation

(b) Tourist camps at Tshoka on the trail

(c) A pristine temperate boradleaved forest at some inaccessable areas of KNP

(d) Alpine scrub land with Rhododendrons, Junipers and the permanent goth at Dzongri

(e) Fuel wood collection by porters at higher elevations has been one of the major sources of habitat destruction

(f) Tree fodder collection: a daily schedule of the locals

Plate 3

(a) Pack animals grazing and trampling along the trail

(b) Livestock grazing on the Khecheopalri lake

(c) Habitat degradation along the trail are responsible for trail errosion

(d) Non-biodegradable garbage disposal near a campsite on the trail

(e) Participatory Rural Appraisal excercise at the Yuksam village

(f) Participatory Rural Appraisal excercise at the Khecheopalri village

Plate 4

(a) Clean-up campaign in Yuksam village

(b) Clean-up campaign in the Khecheopalri lake surroundings by involving local community

(c) Awareness drive for porters

(d) Skill development training for hotel/ lodge woners in Yuksam village

(e) Exchange of experiences and experties; Travel Agent Association of Sikkim (TAAS) and Travel Agent Association of Nepal (TAAN)